Death of the Good Doctor

LESSONS FROM THE HEART
OF THE AIDS EPIDEMIC

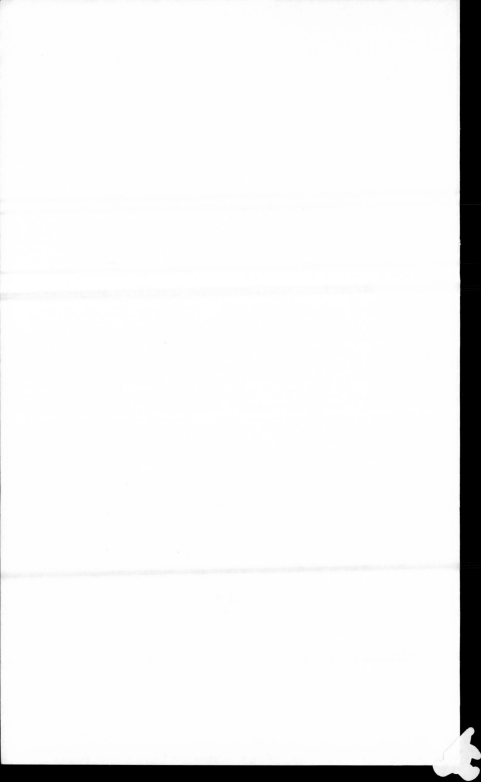

Death of the Good Doctor

LESSONS FROM THE HEART
OF THE AIDS EPIDEMIC

KATE SCANNELL

CLEIS

Life?
Well, it's stories.
Lots of stories.

—ELLA RITER

Published in the United States by Cleis Press Inc.,
P.O. Box 14684, San Francisco, California 94114.

Printed in the United States.
Cover design: Scott Idleman
Cover photo: Melanie Friend
Text design: Karen Huff
Cleis Press logo art: Juana Alicia
First Edition
10 9 8 7 6 5 4 3 2 1

Library of Congress Cataloging-in Publication Data

Scannell, Kate
    Death of the good doctor : lessons from the heart of the AIDS epidemic /
Kate Scannell. — 1st ed.
    p.   cm.
    ISBN 1-57344-091-4 (alk. paper)
    1. Scannell, Kate.   2. AIDS (disease)—California—Alameda County
Biography.   3. Physicians—California—Alameda County Biography.
I. Title.
RC607.A26 S27   1999
362.1'969792'0092—dc21
    [B]   99-40524
                                                       CIP

"Death of the Good Doctor" first appeared as "Skills and Pills"
in *AIDS: The Women,* copyright © 1988 by Ines Rieder and Patricia Ruppelt.
Copyright reassigned in 1996 to Kate A. Scannell by Cleis Press.
"Sleeping with the Fishes" first appeared in *Alligator Juniper* in Summer 1999.

This book is dedicated
with deep affection and gratitude
to my patients,
present and gone.

Acknowledgments

I wish to thank Diane Buczek for her clear eyes and open heart, which have been both beacon and shelter for me. I want to express to her my deepest gratitude for the steadfast patience and careful attention with which she chooses to brave the depths and uncertainties with me.

For standing fearless with me in the dark, over and over, I am profoundly grateful to Mardy Ireland.

I thank my parents, Norma and Jack, for allowing me to begin my life with them. And to return home, again and again.

I would like to acknowledge the amazing people and coworkers who were the heart and soul of our AIDS services: Viola Mehrten and Ann deCourcey, Sonia Burns, Barbara Johnson, Jo Cardoza, Olive Munro, Linda Redford, Patti Rose, Carolyn Smith, Derek Kerr, Craig Lindquist, Mrs. Harris, Wayne Rodrigues, Lori Franks, Bonnie Mager, Deana LeDeux, Don DeMorrow, Bob Read, Helen Morton, and Jim Row. I want to thank them for their craziness, their humanity, their intelligence, their bravery, their ability to stay open to pain and love, and all the times we fell apart a little and came back together again.

Les Solomon, I love you dearly for your comforting humor and your medical mind, which were always steadying during the whirligig beginning. For their considerate administrative and practical support for the ward, I would like to express appreciation to James Richardson and Michael Smart. Zee Wong, thank you for your support and friendship during the hard times. Leslie Martin and Pansy Kwong—your encouragement was invaluable. Joan King-Angell, Karen Axelsson, Betty Lee, Tom Ewing, Signa and Jenny and Bea, and Sharon Lojun—thanks for being such great doctors for me.

I am indebted to my agent, Andrée Abecassis, for her faith in my writing; to Felice Newman and Stephen Lehman for their kind and skillful editing; and to Frédérique Delacoste for her enthusiasm. Thanks also to Mimi Kusch for her careful copyediting.

I am grateful to the hospital grounds crew who carefully maintained the beauty of the courtyard garden. To Teresa Anderson and other members of the utilization review office for their exceedingly benevolent reign. To Nancie Glenk-Janiak and the medical transcriptionists who patiently tolerated my lengthy dictations of patients' stories into the medical record. To Nóírín Ní Riain, for the light in her songs.

I also wish to acknowledge the pioneering courage and generosity of the Center for AIDS Services, the AIDS Project, the Steamworks Baths, the Massage Project, and the man who played Chuckles the Clown at the annual AIDS picnics.

Foremost, I wish to thank the people on the ward—patients, friends, and family—who opened their hearts and shared their stories with me. I am deeply grateful to them. I want them to know how they echo within me still.

Kate Scannell
July 1999

Contents

Introduction

In 1985 ours was one of two hospitals in northern California to create an inpatient AIDS ward. Fairmont Hospital, a 120-year-old facility originally serving as a tuberculosis sanatorium, saw its doors open to another modern-day epidemic with the emergence of AIDS in the 1980s. Backed by funding from the Alameda County Health Care Service Agency, the hospital remodeled one medical ward, the "B2 ward," to provide a space dedicated to AIDS patients. In this early phase of the epidemic, the creation of a special ward seemed prudent: it allowed camaraderie and safety for a population of patients who were often branded as highly contagious (and sometimes intentional) vectors of a rapidly fatal infection that additionally carried the social stigmata of male homosexuality or drug use. The ward also facilitated expertise of medical care and ensured that the small group of health-care workers willing to work with AIDS patients was assigned to cover shifts. Members of the local gay community served as fund-raisers and policy advisers in the ward's development, and their continued presence on the ward promoted the patients' trust.

Twenty miles away and across the Bay Bridge, San Francisco General Hospital provided a remarkable medical model of expert and compassionate AIDS care. I had been working in its research facility and medical clinic since 1983, watching the mystery of AIDS unfold within the dependable hands of a few doctors, notably, Paul Volberding, Donald Abrams, and Constance Wofsy.

Because ours was one of two regional hospitals in the early 1980s with a designated inpatient AIDS ward, we provided care to men and women from a wide geographic base who looked to us as a sort of medical enclave. As a county facility, we also served a largely indigent population—some born into poverty and others newly impoverished by AIDS. Our patients reflected the varied ethnic and racial diversity characteristic of Alameda County, California—an East Bay region encompassing Oakland and Berkeley.

The broad mix of humanity congregating on our ward through the common denominator of a lethal infection created a unique community of people—rich and poor, men and women, socially privileged and socially outcast, gay and straight and everything in between. Our disparate lives constellated quickly around the sudden emergence of an epidemic that, like Camus' Plague, "crashed down on our heads" from a blue sky, and many of us who would otherwise be strangers found ourselves linked together by a submicroscopic virus.

I consider the five years I served as the ward's clinical director to be the period of my life in which I held most fully the stunning complexity and extraordinary richness of the world. In 1985 I stumbled into this position with a stuttering grace, an ambivalence about working with the dying, and a dread of caring for injection drug users. When I left in 1990, I felt as though I had experienced, for the first time, genuine gratitude and profound joy in my work as a physician. These I discovered by walking into a succession of individual lives on the ward that shook me, stunned me, alarmed me, twisted me, righted me, tricked me, and amazed me. The experience has influenced me professionally beyond the wisdom of libraries and lecture halls.

As I write this, there still exists appreciable misunderstanding about AIDS and social stigma against people with HIV infection. But it is also true that these problems are not the same as they were at the beginning of the epidemic. Because my patients' stories occurred within a historical context unique to the earliest years of the epidemic, because much of how they suffered their disease was rooted in the sociopolitical climate of the 1980s, I think it is important to remember some of that early history. I offer here a personalized account of the time, illustrated with a selection of newspaper and journal clippings I saved. Randy Shilts' extraordinary book, *And the Band Played On,* should be consulted by anyone wishing to study the global history and politics of the early epidemic.

When I was six years old, I had a dream in which I ran to a house several yards away at the end of an old stone walkway. But when I arrived at the house and opened its front door, the house moved farther down the walkway. I ran to it again. And again. Each time I was about to step over the door's threshold, the house moved farther away. I occasionally looked back to see the increasingly long distance that I had traveled, and then I'd proceed forward once more. But at some point, I stopped running—I ambled or strolled toward the house instead. I do not now recall if I ever entered the house in my dream.

When I think about my overall experience in AIDS work, I often recall this dream. In the early years of the epidemic, it seemed as though we all kept running toward some threshold of understanding AIDS and finding its cure, generally to discover that the threshold would suddenly shift again. I remember multiple disappointments at the door, multiple failures of "cures" like AL-721, ampli-gen, disulfurim, antisense hybridons, BHT, carrisyn, coenzyme Q, compound Q, dextran sulfate, fusidic acid, HPA-23, hypericin, interferon, Iscador, isoprinosine, nal-trexone, ozone, passive immunotherapy, peptide T, ribavirin. By 1990, I stopped running to the door; I had learned to walk cautiously through the domain of AIDS and I adopted a sobriety about expecting cures.

In the 1980s, it was not unusual for physicians and nurses to refuse to care for AIDS patients. Many patients were admitted to our ward after their health-care providers abandoned them once they were diagnosed with AIDS. Heated debates occurred within the medical community and respectable medical journals over whether or not physicians, nurses, and dentists were obligated to provide care for people with HIV. In 1987 we read "Patients Without Physicians: The New Risk of AIDS" in the *Journal of the American Medical Association*; we learned from the *American Medical News* that one fourth of the residents surveyed at New York City hospitals believed it was not unethical to refuse care for patients with AIDS; *Internal Medicine* reported that, among more than 4,100 medical internists surveyed nationally, 54 percent believed they had the right to refuse treatment to AIDS patients; and the American Dental Association released a study showing that almost four out of five dentists would refuse to treat anyone testing positive for the AIDS virus.

In 1988 California's first lawsuit over whether doctors and dentists could refuse to work on patients with HIV was filed in San Francisco Superior Court. That same year we saw corporations raise prices for vinyl exam gloves from thirty-two to thirty-six dollars a case to around eighty dollars.

The debates continued, and in 1989, from a series of letters to the editor in the prestigious *New England Journal of Medicine,* we read the rhetoric commonly spoken but rarely written so unapologetically: "Pious statements from higher-ups like the Surgeon General... about the treatment of patients with AIDS do not cut it. It is one thing to treat a patient with AIDS and quite another to come into direct contact with that patient's blood.... You cannot command people not to be afraid. Fear is not logical and does not take orders.... No one, from the Surgeon General on down to the most liberal human rights lawyers, can condemn a doctor for not taking on a patient with AIDS...if that action truly stems from fear. It does not matter whether the belief is rational or irrational, as long as it is true."

That same year, one of my patients, returning from a trip to his homeland, gave me a news clipping from the *Kuwait Times* (Zul Haj, "Al Fatwa to Discuss Proposal on AIDS Victims," 5 July 1989, sec. 3, p. 1409): "The Al-Fatwa House in Kuwait is to discuss the suggestion made by the head of the Fatwa Committee at Cairo's Al-Azhar University on Monday that all AIDS victims should be killed....Abdullah Al-Mashad...said AIDS patients should be denied food, water, and medical treatment." This same patient had been denied medical care in his rural California community.

In 1989 I became personally embroiled in the debates after publishing an article in *The Journal of Acquired Immunodeficiency Syndromes* dispelling a common excuse or unfounded fear invoked by some surgeons to rationalize withholding surgeries from HIV-infected patients. Months earlier, I had received a call from a distraught woman whose asymptomatic HIV-infected husband was being denied life-saving cardiac surgery at another hospital. The surgeons explained that they "suspected" his immune system could be further damaged by the stress of surgery; they insisted that they were "merely concerned" for his well-being.

I told the woman that no data existed supporting the surgeons' notion and that I had heard that same mythical postulate used to withhold therapeutic or palliative surgery from other HIV-infected people. The woman's call prompted me to research the medical literature and publish my report dispelling the surgeons' myth. Subsequently, I received many angry and disagreeable (all anonymous) letters from surgeons across the country; fortunately, they were outnumbered by those from patients and physicians (including surgeons) who were able to use the article to negotiate surgical care of patients in their communities.

Occasionally in the mid-eighties we admitted frail, terminally ill people whose families had provided them a one-way bus or plane ticket directing them to our ward. We also admitted many patients who had waited until becoming desperately ill with advanced HIV disease before seeking medical care because they feared their jobs would be terminated should their employers or coworkers realize—or even suspect—that they were HIV infected. Incredibly, in 1986, the U.S Justice Department stated that an employer's *irrational* fear of AIDS spreading in the workplace *would justify* job discrimination. Accordingly, we saw hard-working men and women—teachers, cooks, clerks, accountants—fired from jobs because their employers or coworkers feared that somehow the individual posed a threat of AIDS.

In 1987, 25 percent of physicians in one large poll believed that employers should be allowed to ban employees with AIDS from the workplace, and Senator Jesse Helms recommended a quarantine of people testing positive for HIV. In 1988, Georgia Tech's Center for Work Performance Problems gauged that two thirds of workers in the United States would be "concerned" about sharing a restroom at work with an AIDS-afflicted colleague; 40 percent of workers had reservations about sharing cafeteria facilities with AIDS patients, and 37 percent would not share tools or equipment with them. A nationwide survey in 1989 reported that 45 percent of respondents believed that HIV-infected physicians should be barred from practicing medicine.

In the 1980s HIV-infected people were often denied housing by landlords and families. One of our most difficult dilemmas was the problematic discharge from the hospital of fragile or moderately infirm AIDS patients no longer requiring acute medical care. For years, there were no community or skilled nursing facilities in our local area that accepted boarders with HIV. We were fortunate in the early history of the ward to be able to provide some patients prolonged hospitalizations largely because of the county's administrative uncertainties about managing a new and chaotic epidemic while trying to devise a countywide AIDS program. Consequently, in many instances, homeless, vulnerable patients stayed with us for weeks or months, often up until their deaths. This unusual arrangement, unlikely to be recreated in today's strict cost-containment era, allowed for long, intimate relationships to develop among patients, families, and staff. For this rare opportunity I remain extremely grateful.

Beyond the particular fears of AIDS in the medical office, home, or workplace, the early period of the epidemic was also characterized by a generalized hysteria surrounding people with HIV, mostly mythological imaginings that they possessed unlimited power—and even the desire—to spread AIDS to others. In this regard, my most telling personal experience involved a million-dollar lawsuit initiated against me and the ward in 1986 by a man whose fiancée had abandoned him after discovering that he had taken a bath in a tub that was also used by AIDS patients. Although the man did not contract HIV, he insisted he was due compensation for his anxiety and emotional distress. While the suit was later dropped, it chilled me to hear the considerable public opinion that considered his claim reasonable.

In the 1980s we encountered morticians refusing to embalm or handle bodies of deceased AIDS patients, schools dismissing children with HIV, a fire department refusing to touch the bloodied body of a dying AIDS patient, hospital cafeteria services refusing to deliver food trays to AIDS patients, an emergency medical unit denying care to a baby with AIDS taken in by a monastery, social clubs for heterosexuals fearful of AIDS and willing to take blood tests every three months to prove they didn't have it. Representative William Dannemeyer introduced a bill that would prohibit anyone with AIDS from working in the health-care industry and deny federal funds to cities that did not bar children with AIDS from public schools. Presidential candidate Lyndon LaRouche's initiative barring people with HIV from teaching or food handling qualified for California's ballot. In 1987 we read a headline in the *Weekly World News:* "Angry Neighbors Kill AIDS Victim—'We told him to move away— he wouldn't listen,' says vigilante."

During these dark times of the 1980s, when people with HIV suffered rapid deaths, rampant discrimination, job and home loss, the punitive assaults of others' irrational fears; when our country was flailing to find a compassionate understanding of the epidemic, political and religious leadership in this country often remained silent on these matters. Many, however, used their voices to thwart safe-sex education programs, to denounce condom use, to blame others for the epidemic across international and religious boundaries, and to condemn outright the people suffering with HIV.

President Ronald Reagan avoided making any public statement about the AIDS epidemic until mid-1985— four years after 12,000 American citizens had been stricken with the disease. In 1987, Secretary of State George Schultz denounced the Soviet government for blaming the AIDS epidemic on the United States, while presidential candidate Lyndon LaRouche charged the Soviet Union with helping to engineer the spread of AIDS in this country.

In 1986 the Los Angeles Roman Catholic Archdiocese withdrew its support for a program endorsing the use of condoms for AIDS prevention because it opposed contraceptives and sex outside marriage. This position was echoed by many Catholic dioceses across the country. A 1987 Gallop Poll reported that 58 percent of evangelicals viewed AIDS as punishment, and 59 percent were inclined to say that victims had only themselves to blame. A year later, southern Baptists adopted a resolution calling homosexuality "an abomination in the eyes of God" and declared that homosexuals were primarily responsible for the spread of AIDS, which not only affected them but also "innocent victims."

There was no one like Magic Johnson yet and, certainly, no Democratic or Republican national convention speaker with AIDS within miles of the popular media in the 1980s. When the movie idol Rock Hudson died on July 25, 1985, his AIDS diagnosis had been successfully concealed from the public ante mortem. In 1987, Liberace's manager angrily denied the "vicious rumor" that his client died of AIDS; one month later, the Riverside County coroner accused the entertainer's doctors of covering up the cause of Liberace's AIDS-related death as heart failure.

On medical fronts, the first blood tests to detect HIV antibodies became available in 1985; health-care workers and patients finally had a tool for resolving uncertainty about an HIV diagnosis. We would also learn of the test's technical fallibilities and its potential abuses by nonmedical interests. In 1985 our naïveté about and our hope for those people who did test positive for HIV were reflected in this statement from the *Journal of the American Medical Association*: "It is hoped that only some people infected with [HIV] will develop overt AIDS... It is unknown whether heterosexual transmission will ever become important in the epidemiology of AIDS in the United States."

As time passed, however, it became evident that HIV transmission through heterosexual sex—as well as blood transfusions and injection drug use—was "important." Two years after HIV tests became available, we knew (from analysis of old, stored blood samples) that 36 percent of people infected for seven years had developed AIDS; so in 1987, we could still hope that the majority of HIV-infected people would not ultimately suffer AIDS. Then, once an AIDS-related infection was diagnosed, life spans were measured in months: six to nine months in 1982 and eleven to fifteen months by 1986.

In the spring of 1987, the FDA approved the first AIDS drug (AZT or azidothymidine, later known as ZDV or zidovudine) for prescription use in the United States. Although not heralded as a cure, AZT was expected to extend a patient's life a few extra months. While this enlivened hope for many, others were unable or unwilling to tolerate its side effects to gain a short reprieve. Additionally, the high cost of AZT was prohibitive for some, and corporate profit-taking was incriminated: reportedly, one day's supply of five AZT capsules contained an estimated fifteen cents' worth of ingredients and cost between one-fifty and two-fifty to manufacture while selling in drugstores for nine dollars; the cost of one year's supply of AZT ran as high as eight thousand dollars.

By 1988, the mean number of months from AIDS diagnosis to death remained fewer than twenty-four, and HIV infection/AIDS had become the third leading cause of death among young adults in the United States. In 1989 the number of AIDS cases in this country reached the 100,000 mark with more than 55,000 deaths, and depressing new data suggested that, ultimately, almost all HIV-infected people would go on to develop AIDS.

By 1990, 100,777 deaths were reported among persons with AIDS in the United States, and one million additional citizens were thought to be infected with HIV. Hard-won progress could be measured on several fronts, as expressed in this excerpt from "AIDS Policies in the 1990s" published in the *Journal of the American Medical Association*:

> More reasons for both optimism and concern in 1990 may be found in an examination of public policy on AIDS... Significant progress has been

made in addressing AIDS and HIV infection in the workplace. The courts have affirmed that a child with AIDS or HIV infection has a right to public education, and in most cases this has meant inclusion of the child in his or her usual classroom. Similarly, the right of employees with AIDS or HIV infection to remain on the job has been repeatedly upheld... Physicians who order HIV antibody tests without patient consent or who misdiagnose or improperly treat HIV-related disease could put themselves at serious risk of litigation. Regarding the issue of a health worker's duty to treat, [the author] affirms the legal responsibility of health workers to not deny care to HIV-infected persons.

At this writing, it has been eighteen years since AIDS was first identified. The number of AIDS cases in the United States has continued to rise, with the Centers for Disease Control (CDC) reporting more than 683,000 cases through December of 1998.

Much of the landscape has shifted. In the early nineties, many politicians began speaking compassionately about AIDS, and countless celebrities donned the red AIDS ribbon in public. 1996 proved to be a pivotal year when, after years of bad news on the medical front, optimism clearly rose at the eleventh annual International Conference on AIDS. Data from various clinical studies using combinations of newer anti-HIV drugs generated hope that effective tools existed to treat and monitor HIV infection. The potent new anti-HIV drugs—nucleoside reverse transcriptase inhibitors, non-nucleoside reverse transcriptase inhibitors, and protease inhibitors—were reported to decrease HIV replication, delay opportunistic infections, enhance immunologic status, and, in some cases, virtually eliminate detection of HIV in patients' bloodstreams. Highly refined and sensitive blood tests that measured a patient's "viral burden" of HIV were developed and found to correlate with the severity of a patient's illness and the efficacy of his or her treatment.

These medical breakthroughs began translating into improved survival rates. Indeed, although the estimated number of deaths from HIV had increased steadily through 1994, it declined for the first time in 1996. In conjunction with preventive therapies to thwart opportunistic infections, use of the newer antivirals was credited with an overall 26 percent decline in AIDS-related deaths among adults aged twenty-five to forty-four years in 1996.

In 1997, the risk of HIV infection from a blood transfusion (as high as one in 100 units in some cities in the early 1980s) fell to one in 680,000 units, women accounted for 20 percent of the nation's AIDS population, and heterosexual transmission became the fastest-growing mode of spread. In the first six months of 1997, AIDS deaths dropped an additional 44 percent in the United States. People responding to the new AIDS treatments began grappling with issues of returning to work. By the late nineties, many AIDS hospices closed, and the number of AIDS hospital admissions continued to decrease. For the first time, in the late nineties, it seemed possible to conceive of AIDS as something other than a quick death sentence. For the first time, we wondered if AIDS might become a chronic treatable illness. After ten years of preparing people to die, we began preparing them to live.

I celebrated 1996. But I, like many of my old colleagues, had run to the door too often to feel confident that we were finally standing at the definitive threshold of a cure. Indeed, one year later, at the end of 1997, hope shifted again: researchers showed us that blood cells taken from patients who had responded to the newer antivirals with no detectable viral loads in their bloodstream could be stimulated to cause HIV to multiply and burst out of those cells. This indicated that HIV could hide within cells for years and threaten to reemerge if antivirals were discontinued. In 1998, up to 20 percent of long-term AIDS patients were found to carry HIV viral strains resistant to the new drug treatments. The cost of the new antivirals—at 1999 Western market prices of a thousand dollars per month—remain prohibitive for people living in Africa and other developing nations where 90 percent of AIDS cases occur.

Today, I look back and note the great distance we have traveled through the painful and mysterious realm of AIDS. I look ahead and wonder what will greet us in the next millennium. Will we find ways to rid the body of latently-infected cells? Will we discover that antiviral treatments should be continued indefinitely? Will prolonged therapy promote drug failures and resistance, or long-term side effects? How will we reconcile the fact that current life-prolonging combination treatments, costing ten to fifteen thousand dollars a year, are made available to people on a socioeconomic—rather than medical—basis?

In 1986, one of my patients, a twenty-two-year-old man dying of AIDS, told me that he wished he could live "just ten more years," to the age of thirty-two. Then thirty-two myself, I asked him, "Why that particular age?" He explained that, by his estimate, it would take at least a decade for the world to arrive at a compassionate under-standing of AIDS and, perhaps, a medical cure. "Besides," he said, "I'd just like to see how a little more of my own life plays out."

Years after this young man's death, new treatments emerged that would have been astounding news to the men and women on our ward who awaited their deaths in the relative hopelessness of the 1980s. If these newer drugs do indeed ultimately translate into long-term management or even cure of AIDS, then it is conceivable that we will never again witness the phenomenon of AIDS wards. This gratifying scenario, possibly just beyond the horizon, casts a somber shadow on the memories of the men and women in my stories who suffered their disease a decade too soon for these discoveries.

LESSONS FROM THE HEART
OF THE AIDS EPIDEMIC

PROLOGUE

"What's in the milk crate?" my friend asked.
"A couple hundred people, all dead," I answered.

In May 1995 my friend's question inspired me to reopen the sealed crate that had been stored in my basement workroom for five years. Within it were over two hundred medical records and dozens of stories I had written while I was clinical director of a county hospital's AIDS ward between 1985 and 1990. Near the crate were three cardboard cartons filled with journals, newspaper clippings, correspondences, and photographs that I had also saved from that experience.

The evening after my friend's inquiry, I went down to my basement and hovered over these boxes. I tried to convince myself that they were best left undisturbed. For half a decade they had survived in the very impractical location at the center of my workroom. I had managed to walk around them and step over them countless times while rummaging through my gardening equipment, woodworking gadgets, and painting tools.

But my friend had me wondering why I had arranged my workspace so that I was forced to orbit around my old patients with every rosebush pruned, wood figure carved, and scene and portrait painted. It seemed as though, unconsciously, I had been circling around my mementos for years, like a plane waiting for clearance to land.

I had taken the crate from my father's house in Detroit in 1971 when I left home. I imagined that it was the crate I had sat on in the back of his milk truck when I accompanied him on his routes as a child. I had dragged that crate with me, through many phases of life, for twenty-four years. Finally, it had ended up in the basement of my California home.

That evening in 1995, I cleared a place on the floor and sat down, alighting alongside my boxes and, throughout the long night, I drew my stories and records from the crate, one by one, touching each of my patients once again. There were Lana and Jay and Susan and Curtis and Elton and Marvin...

I opened the black canvas journal in which I had recorded the day-to-day deaths on the AIDS ward. From it, I read each name aloud into the darkness beyond the small circle of overhead light illuminating my boxes. Each name felt like an invocation, a lamentation, a witnessing of someone's life. And it would take a while—another year or so—before I would fully realize that one of the lives pulled from the crate was my own.

Surprisingly, in the midst of what seemed that night to be an impenetrable grief, I sometimes found myself laughing—as I recalled Jay's schizoid goldfish, the deviant soap opera scripts Yolanda and I created, the baffling etiquette discussions with Elton about dying properly or, with Gregory, appropriate cruising behaviors in front of Mother Teresa. In my dramatic emotional swings that night, I felt like the madwoman in the attic—except that I was in the basement with a couple of hundred other people.

I would spend the next year reshaping the stories of my patients' lives into the collection you now hold in your hands. I would mine my personal journals, remembering what it was like to become a physician in the whirlwind of the early AIDS epidemic and what it was like to be a woman whose experience rubbed up against the traditional narratives of physicians' lives.

Upon completing this project in October 1996, on the eve of my first sabbatical after sixteen years of medical practice, I would discover that I had both uterine and ovarian cancers. Ironically, I would find myself faced with a notoriously lethal cancer in the same year that new, life-prolonging AIDS therapies would emerge. I would listen to bleak and uncertain reports about my own survival. I would reexperience the mystery of human intimacy against the backdrop of life and death from the perspective of a patient. I would invoke the lessons I learned from the heart of the AIDS epidemic to guide me when my own life was pressed against death.

Although some of the pieces in this collection are sobering, others are comical or somewhere in between. I have written them largely out of my desire to give voice to two rarely discussed aspects of a physician's experience: the highly interpersonal dimension of medical practice in which patients and physicians mutually affect each other and the uniquely personal dimension of one physician's voice, a woman's voice, that expands the traditional physician narrative.

These stories are anchored within my relationships to individual patients through whom the vast complexities of the early AIDS epidemic were filtered and uniquely focused. They relate the often miraculous ways by which our lives converged, causing me to stumble into grace, into unexplored territories of my soul, into an expanded understanding of my patients and of myself as physician. They concern people connecting and disconnecting with one another. They describe myriad ways of dying. They relate what happened when patients shared their lives with me. They describe the foundations of my experience with my patients, which ultimately helped me to accept and endure my own cancer.

Our stories occurred between 1985 and 1990 at Fairmont Hospital, a public institution in Alameda County, California, which had established the second inpatient AIDS ward (after San Francisco General Hospital) in northern California. The names and identifying features of patients and staff have been changed to honor people's privacy.

I have been told that this collection of stories and essays is difficult to categorize because its themes span general human interest, cultural studies, medicine, death, coming-of-age stories, AIDS studies, lesbian and gay studies, feminism, and spirituality; its format and style range from those of the short story, the personal essay, creative nonfiction, and memoir.

And I would have to agree with those comments. I would have to say that my experience unfolded precisely in those ways.

Death of the Good Doctor

There are some things you learn best in calm,
and some in storm.
—WILLA CATHER, THE SONG OF THE LARK

We died together. It was January 1986.

Four months earlier I had accepted the job that would introduce us to each other. It was offered in the local classifieds as: "Wanted—General internist. Inpatient service at county hospital. Community setting."

It sounded perfect. I had spent the last three years as a physician and research fellow at San Francisco General Hospital during the chaotic and ominous emergence of the AIDS epidemic. It had arrived mysteriously, as a few dead bodies lying in a mute shadow. As that shadow enlarged and darkened the landscape, as the deaths multiplied, everyone scrambled for understanding. Our clinics increasingly tended to the people who stood before us, panicking, pointing to evidence that their bodies had been branded by the deadly plague, begging us to intervene.

By 1985 I desperately wanted to escape the increasing domination of AIDS in my clinical practice and personal life. Although reluctant to leave the intellectually stimulating environment of the university and the vibrant beauty of San Francisco, I informed my department chairman of my decision to investigate the county hospital job. He replied, "Kate, I think it's a *big mistake*. Your academic career will take a nose dive."

Two weeks later I was in my research lab preparing for my nose dive. I packed my small cache of personal belongings in a cardboard box that had served previously to transport flammable solvents. I took my melon-red seat cushion, my shamrock-studded coffee mug, my impressive collection of magic markers, and my medical textbooks. After surrendering my research log to a colleague, I said good-bye to my coworkers and slowly walked the long corridor toward the exit. There, on the wall before the doorway, was a larger-than-life portrait of the actress Rosalind Russell. (She had been a primary benefactor of the research facility.) I looked into her eyes, my cardboard box unwieldy in my hands, and spoke to her one final time. "Well, Roz, I guess this is good-bye."

Several weeks later I began my new job. I had visited the site twice before, for brief interviews with John, the medical director. The hospital stood in stark contrast to the modern, angular design of San Francisco General with its vertical reach. Built in 1864 in classic California mission style as a series of white adobe buildings with clay-tile roofs, it sprawled horizontally across beautifully landscaped grounds. It did straddle a fault line in the East Bay hills—a fact I elected to ignore.

On my first day of work, one of the physicians approached me, shook my hand vigorously, and said, "Boy, am I happy that *you're* here."

I was pleased and mildly flattered, assuming that his comment reflected admiration of my academic credentials.

"Thank you," I replied, demurely.

However, his next remark suggested something different. "It's a tremendous relief to have you take charge of the AIDS patients. They're such a handful."

Stunned, I replied, "Wait. What do you mean? That's not why I'm here."

He grimaced. "Oh. Well, that's what John told me. He said he hired you because of your AIDS experience at San Francisco General. He said you'd be the director of our new AIDS ward."

"No. That's a mistake!" I insisted. "I'm no expert. One of the very reasons I left San Francisco was to get away from AIDS..."

"Listen, Kate, I'm very sorry," he interrupted as his beeper sounded. "I have to answer this call. You'll need to straighten this out with John."

Alarmed and apprehensive about the misunderstanding, I scheduled an appointment with John as soon as he returned from leave. Reluctantly, I walked to the AIDS ward to acquaint myself with those patients already assigned to my medical service. My former chairman's parting words echoed in my head as I began my rounding.

In San Francisco I had worked exclusively in the clinics, with AIDS patients who were still ambulatory, not yet so debilitated. I was unprepared for the mass agony, the staggering casualties before me. I was unnerved by the fact that so many beds were occupied by men and women about my age—in their thirties and forties. Already they were dying, accelerated through time to their twilight years. Their youth made it seem as though a horrible blunder, a sinister foul-up, had wrongly placed them here.

Throughout the first few weeks, my patients overwhelmed me—with their suffering, their dramatic and perplexing diseases, their awesome psychological and emotional needs, and, above all, their dying. I was frightened by the futile desperation of many who wanted to be made well again and to survive that which could not be survived. Often I felt helpless. I thought that the best I could offer these patients was my "cutting-edge" experience with AIDS treatments and the knowledge I had accumulated through years of academically invigorated medical training.

I soon established a routine, beginning my hospital rounds with the non-AIDS patients, because that work was largely containable. Later I could spend what seemed like endless hours on the AIDS ward, trying to locate origins for occult fevers, treat exotic infections, administer chemotherapies, perform lumbar punctures, and counsel distraught lovers and families.

Gradually, my confidence grew. I stalked the AIDS ward like a weary but seasoned gunfighter, ready for medical challenges to present themselves; I would shoot them down with my skills and pills. Diseases that defied my treatments and patients who expired were my valiantly fought failures. No one died because I neglected to offer him or her aggressive, full-service, state-of-the-art care. I became such a sharpshooter for HIV-related problems that AIDS patients gravitated to my medical service.

The emaciation of my patients often reminded me of the disturbing photographs of Buchenwald and Auschwitz prisoners I had seen as a young girl in our family's *Funk and Wagnalls* encyclopedia. Patients with Kaposi's sarcoma who were horribly disfigured by coarse, bulky masses of purple skin tumors regularly disturbed me. One such patient's tumors shoved his eye forward, out of its socket, and his visage caused me to have a recurrent nightmare of the hunchback of Notre Dame.

The AIDS ward generated countless depressing stories and morbid events. I rarely discussed them with even my closest friends, and I never tried to explain how the cumulative deaths might be affecting me. In part, I hesitated to be too grim; but more fundamentally, I was incapable of fully understanding and articulating my own experiences.

Four months passed like this. One day, Manuel, a twenty-two-year-old man with Kaposi's sarcoma, was admitted to the ward. He arrived as a huge, bloated, violaceous, knobby mass with eyelids so swollen that he could no longer see. His dense purple tumors had infiltrated multiple lymph nodes throughout his body, and two had perforated the roof of his mouth. One imposing mass extended from the bottom of his foot so that he could no longer walk. Massive amounts of fluids surrounded and compressed his lungs, making his breathing laborious. Tears literally squeezed through the slits between his puffy eyelids. One of the first things Manuel said to me was, "Doctor, please help me."

Immediately I invoked the certain, sage voices of teachers who had prodded me through ten years of medical training. I dutifully remembered their instructions to remedy this man's troubled breathing. To determine the precise cause and correct therapy for his anemia. To rebalance his wayward electrolytes. To relieve his massive swelling with diuretic medications. I heard the venerable voices of my professors review with me the latest salvage therapies for Kaposi's sarcoma. After all, Manuel had asked me to help him.

So I stuck several needles into his veins and arteries to obtain more medical data about his condition. I inserted an intravenous line through one of the few places on his arm unaffected by firm swelling or rocky, plum-colored tumors. As I placed a plastic cannula into his nose to offer him more oxygen, Manuel looked at me and, again, said, "Doctor, please help me."

I gave him extra potassium through his intravenous line. I connected a blood transfusion bag. Hours later, I finally rested and assured Manuel that his medical problems were being assessed and treated. I told him that we could discuss chemotherapy options in the morning after he was stabilized.

When I left the ward that night, my heart ached for Manuel's suffering. I was exhausted by the demands of his care, but I felt confident that I truly had given him my "all." I felt grateful to be part of a system that could offer state-of-the-art AIDS care to a poor, socially disenfranchised man without medical insurance.

The next morning I arrived at work and discovered that Manuel had died. A night-shift nurse informed me that the evening-duty physician had been summoned to Manuel's bedside hours earlier. The nurse said that Manuel had simply asked that doctor to help him. The physician responded by discontinuing the intravenous fluid and potassium, canceling all lab tests, and terminating the blood transfusion. The physician gave Manuel additional morphine. The nurse said that Manuel smiled and thanked the doctor for helping him. He died within an hour, finally freed from his suffering.

It's stunning how, in the flash of a moment, much of what you think you know and believe can turn on itself so abruptly, so seamlessly, that you don't even have time to feel dizzy or to experience the movement of traveling from one position to its distant, polar opposite. There I was, at Manuel's empty bed, instantly recognizing my wrong-headedness through the actions of the night-duty physician. My entire body cringed and my soul clenched as I imagined Manuel's agony sustained through my unconscious denial of his dying. I looked at my hands with horror, asking myself, What have I done? My shame and regret were unspeakable. Weeks passed before I could face the night-call doctor and thank him for helping Manuel—and me.

Years later I continue to think of Manuel often, and I ask him to forgive me. I tell him that I have never practiced medicine in the same way since his death. After Manuel's disease-ridden corpse finally released his spirit, the classical breeding and customary garb of my traditional medical training fell off me like tattered rags. I began learning—how to recognize the sound of my own voice, listen to my patients, validate the insistent stirrings of my compassionate sensibilities.

As in an archeological expedition, I have tried to reclaim parts of myself that were buried beneath the rubble of the failed structure, the flawed foundation of the medical model I had lived and experienced. I have tried to reintegrate those parts and bring others to consciousness. I have turned the rubble over in my hands, examining it for clues, trying to understand what happened to me during my all-consuming medical training, a time during which I strove earnestly, exhaustively, to become a "good physician" in the conventional Western mode.

Some of the rubble I can identify as remnants of that conventional structure: the trend toward increasing technological interventions; the overriding philosophy that competent physicians save lives, not "lose" them; the blatant chastisement and devaluation of physicians who use their empathy and intuitive insights when interacting with patients; the taboo against using compassion as a diagnostic and therapeutic medical skill.

The "good doctor" in me died with Manuel. January 1986.

Shortly after Manuel's death, I embraced the position of clinical director of the AIDS ward. Subsequently, the targets for my diagnostic sharpshooting became clearer, redefined. A lightness and joy imbued my work. AIDS no longer frightened me, and I rarely had nightmares. I stood the bedside deathwatch frequently, with only a small arsenal of pills.

I learned how to substitute ice cream and French bakery products as principal or even sole therapy for some AIDS patients with "complex medical problems." I officially prescribed sunshine, a trip to a local department store, an afternoon with a tomcat, and massage as "primary" treatments for others. For weeks on daily rounds I visited a demented AIDS patient who believed that he was back on his Texas ranch tending his beloved pigs and chickens; for days we discussed the problems posed by a few errant hogs and the most lucrative schemes to market fresh eggs. Once we invited the neighbors/patients on the ward for a farm-style breakfast in his room. This man never saw a needle in his arms or a catheter in his veins. I believe he was peaceful and free of pain when he died.

Just as each individual with AIDS may experience his or her illness in stages of the Kübler-Ross scheme, as a physician I have responded similarly to the total specter of AIDS. Writing this years later, I am moving between grief and acceptance of this disease, and I am comfortable now reconciling reality with hope. After a dark period of responding to so much suffering and death with unmitigated grief and defiance, I have been able finally to find some peace, walking more comfortably, day-to-day, alongside the certainty of my own death. And I am grateful to hear my own voice once again and to feel the renewed strength of my compassionate sensibilities.

I think of Manuel often.

The First Long Week

Oh, Lucy, what are we going to do now?
— Ethel Mertz, as played by Vivian Vance, in I Love Lucy

I can't believe I got myself into this mess. The AIDS ward is so chaotic and, like most of the staff, I feel as though we're in a constant maelstrom. We've encountered a new psychosocial issue or policy decision to reconcile every day. On uncertain terrain and without clear direction, we are trying to plant our feet on common, solid ground. And the patients—they're an endless sorrow. Their illnesses are enormous, their needs are overwhelming, and their deaths hover like specters beside them. They are largely impoverished or disenfranchised, and we have no social agencies offering them housing or hospice services.

It seems much longer than just one month ago that I was sitting in my research lab with an endless cup of coffee, leisurely waiting for regimented timers to direct me to the next step in my experiments. To a precise measure of powdery chemical here, a beaker of solvent there, a brisk stir of potion with a glass rod clinking against the flask, a whir and spin in the centrifuge, and an overnight respite in the incubator. The unknowns pulled together so neatly in the mornings, becoming knowable with scientific accuracy, ticking rhythmically from the scintillation counter, through the printer, and into orderly rows of numbers on long, white strips of paper.

Karl, the first patient I met this week, was a furious, bitter man who told me outright, unapologetically, that he had thrown a tub of his pee at one of the night-shift doctors days before. "I threw it at the asshole. It took him three days to get me something for these sores on my leg. That fucker won't mess with me anymore."

Karl weighed only seventy-five pounds, and his dense, unfocused anger seemed to account for much of his weight. I listened to his tempestuous rantings for nearly an hour. He claimed that AIDS was the most horrific event in the "entire history of the world," that people were fundamentally ruthless and insensitive, that physicians and nurses were complete idiots, that the whole of society was savage and corrupt, that the pharmaceutical industry was thoroughly sinister. He declared, "No one gives a damn about me because I'm of no material value to anyone."

That so much vitriol could be contained within the shrunken space of his body amazed me. Nearing the end of our time together, his rage crescendoed and he repeated his telling of the urine escapade, ostensibly as a warning to me. I sat before Karl, dodging his occasional spittle, becoming increasingly fearful of his anger and his lawless behavior. I found myself longing for the serenity and safety of my research lab. The orderly rows of toxic chemicals on shelves above my desk, the shiny metal canisters of radioactive particles, the caustic solutions stoppered in soft-shouldered glass jars, the corrosive acids within beautiful amber bottles—all that lethal beauty and bridled peril seemed a safer haven than the bedside of this man who persisted in dumping his wounded life on me, ramming every poisoned ingredient of his experience into the small space between us. Several times I imagined his blue tub of urine sailing overhead, spilling in flight, showering me and the room like acid rain or radioactive fallout.

Finally walking out his door, I thought, my God, he's dying like this—isolated, bitter, narcissistic, furious. I had never met someone facing death with such violent unhappiness. I envisioned the four chambers within his heart as cold, dark caves of unexplored territory, and my own heart ached for his emptiness.

Jay occupied the next room. A crimson pirate ship sailed on his muscular back, blue roses trellised his ribs, and large-breasted women twined around his hairy arms and pasty thighs. The track marks on his biceps were so prominent that I mistook them for knobbed ropes ensnaring the poor women tattooed there. He sported a razor-sharp crew cut, and his eyes were the blue of frozen lakes. Alongside him in bed sat his languid, fragmented-looking girlfriend. I suspect that they were shooting heroin in his room. They responded to my greeting and inquires as though I were speaking a foreign language in another time zone.

The third patient I met was Lana. She lay in the corner room, propped up in bed, staring at a muted ceiling-mounted television set. After introducing myself, I asked her what she was watching.

"Nothing," she replied flatly. Then, following a deep sigh, "I'm really just waiting to die, is all."

Lana had suffered a debilitating stroke after a clump of bacteria broke free from her infected heart valve and traveled through her blood stream to her brain, clogging the artery that enabled her to move her left arm and leg. Her valve continued to usher periodic waves of emigrant bacteria from its surface to other sites throughout her body, creating a pneumonia in her lungs or an abscess on her leg. Lana also suffered various infections associated with her AIDS. Because of her multiple, advanced ailments and her self-proclaimed intention to continue injecting drugs, surgeons decided that Lana was a "bad candidate" for operative removal of her infected valve.

So Lana was just biding time, waiting for one of her illnesses to usher her through her final exit. Most likely it would be her heart escorting her to a sudden death, with each beat, each violent snap and quake of her diseased valve threatening to dispatch a deadly emissary through her arteries.

In the middle of my first long week on the AIDS ward, I stood alone in the hallway one evening, trying to motivate myself to finish rounding on my service of patients. I felt as though I were struggling to move through a dark node of sadness and doubt that threatened to immobilize me. Already this place had become for me the seed of nightmares. Illnesses were not clearly labeled. Lives were not neatly contained within pretty bottles. Poisons rained free upon the landscape from soaring urinals or bitter deaths. There were no timers dictating rhythm or step. I said to myself, oh, my God, this new job is surely my big mistake.

I leaned against my chart rack, wondering if I were too weak of heart or character or intellect to be physician to these suffering lives and tattered souls. Then, while trying to invoke the momentum to pull me through my remaining rounds, the conversation within my head slowly quieted and yielded to the conversation that seemed to be echoing through the hallway. Listening attentively, I then realized that most of the patients on the ward were watching *I Love Lucy.*

The amplified voices of Lucy and Ethel began filtering into my solitude through the lips of a half-dozen doorways. "Oh, Lucy, what are we going to do now?"

A strange counsel. A peculiar oracle, echoing predicament and uncertainty and journey.

Sleeping with the Fishes

Always chance is powerful.
Always let your hook be cast.
In the pool where you least expect it,
there will be a fish.
—OVID, ARS AMATORIA

Jay. A strange name for such a wan, brutish creature. At twenty-four years of age he was meeting his death in a small corner room on the AIDS ward.

He was a "difficult patient,"someone with major behavioral problems, someone unlikable. He was junk-yard-dog mean, vulgar, crude, self-centered, deceitful, vinegary, and prejudiced. His limbs were as narrow as his reach into the world. Though so young, he was already crusty with emotional scars. Hard plaques, formed by too many heroin needles, comprised his skin and literalized his armored existence. People tended to bounce off the rough, resilient surface of his life: an overtaxed mother who abandoned him to his aunt's care so she could discover life in a trailer park in Arkansas; an alcoholic father who suc-cumbed to liver cirrhosis when Jay was four years old; a disillusioned, abused wife who divorced him because her fragile jaw couldn't sustain another rupture by his fist. I never knew why the army had discharged him. His land-lord had recently evicted him from a decrepit studio apartment in the bad part of town.

Jay referred to his situation poetically as that of a "lone wolf."

I had barely survived unscathed caring for Jay twice before. Once, I treated him for pneumonia and another time for a blood-stream infection he had caused with a dirty needle. During those hospitalizations, he was frequently absent from his room for prolonged periods, missing antibiotic administrations. Reappearing later on the ward, he'd look befuddled and glassy-eyed.

The most wearisome aspect of Jay's behavior was his relentless abuse of the staff and other ward patients, his obscene insults and caustic provocations. He freely expressed misogynist views and a wide variety of racial prejudices. The staff's fervent wishes for Jay's speedy recovery were rarely altruistic.

I didn't like him. Not one bit. Not a single oily strand of his tangled hair. Most of all, I hated the way that I experienced myself in his presence, as somewhat less than fully human, lacking any compassion for him. Around him I felt guarded, diminished, violated, resentful, angry, and afraid. Consciously I tried not to despise him and would have settled for a sense of detachment and equanimity. I was disconcerted, uncertain how to doctor him. I thought that all I might be capable of managing successfully were the cold mechanics of treating his illnesses from a safe personal distance.

While I was away on Christmas leave, Jay had returned to our ward. The glow of my Yuletide cheer fizzled immediately when I spotted his medical chart on my ward rack. Jay had been admitted via the emergency room with a diagnosis of "total body pain." The attending physician had disbursed hefty amounts of narcotics to relieve Jay's global discomfort. A barrage of tests had failed to uncover a physical cause for his generalized agony or spiking fevers. The physician's records suggested that Jay had complied with laboratory and radiologic examinations in exchange for escalating doses of analgesics.

Reluctantly resuming his care, I found him zonked out in bed, ostensibly numbed by the ample doses of narcotics he had received for his "total body pain." I sat alongside him and watched him doze. Occasionally, he moaned and his scrawny limbs twitched. His breathing was slow and deep, interspersed with grand, arching sighs.

The chart notes from the day before indicated that Jay's right lung had collapsed and that he had refused a chest tube to reexpand it. Although lab tests revealed severe anemia, Jay had declined blood transfusions because of his "religious beliefs."

I closed Jay's chart and studied him again. During his intake assessment the previous year, he had informed me that he rejected all things spiritual. "Fuckin' waste of time" is how he referred to the realm of the gods. I now wondered nervously—what he meant by "religious beliefs"; in California, this could refer to a vast array of proclivities and inclinations.

I decided to wake him. With repeated nudging, he finally roused from his narcosis. After his eyeballs aligned and registered my presence, he grinned and managed, "Hey, doc."

"Hi, Jay," I replied, somewhat guarded. "Looks like you've had a couple of interesting weeks here."

"I've had more interesting times in my life," he slurred. "This wasn't no big deal."

He clutched his right side while struggling to sit upright in bed, becoming short of breath from the effort.

"Jay," I said, "what's this business about total body pain?"

"Oh, man, I was just hurting. You know, all over," he mumbled. "Everywhere."

"Yes," I replied, "I see that you've become the new record holder for narcotic consumption in this hospital."

He was silent.

"Even your toes?" I asked.

"Yeah, my toes hurt."

"Your uvula, too?"

"Yeah, doc."

"And your tremboid?"

"Yeah, bad," he replied.

"Jay," I said, "there's no such thing as a tremboid."

He shook his head and muttered, "Shit, man. It would be hurting if there was."

Because we were a county facility, many of our patients were poor, uneducated, and socially disenfranchised injection drug users, or "IDUs." They tended to be difficult to treat for a variety of reasons, but most problematic was their often singular focus on drug procurement in the hospital. It was wondrous sometimes to watch a person like Jay bend all forms of human interaction into one shape—a drug negotiation.

"Well, we're going to have to remedy this ridiculous overmedication," I said. "Since there are enough issues to deal with today, let's discuss this first thing in the morning."

"If I'm awake," he sniggered.

"Well," I said, "if you wish to stay asleep during the discussion, that's fine—I can have it without you. There'd probably be less argument. I do hope that you're alert enough to realize that I know there's no way you could tolerate this much narcotic unless you'd been 'practicing' beforehand." I generally made a point of verbalizing the obvious to the IDUs because they often held the bizarre view that a "nice girl" like me couldn't see the proverbial pig on a sofa. Their magical thinking held that someone outside their drug culture couldn't possibly recognize manipulative behavior or the significance of a dirty syringe in the wastebasket.

Jay laughed and then stabilized his chest with his hand to suppress the cough and pain that followed. When he calmed down he said, "Yeah, well, I guess I've been using some." Before I could respond, he grinned and added, "But I stopped a few years ago, if I remember correctly."

"Yeah, right," I replied, rolling my eyes. "I see we'll have to develop this story later. Perhaps when you're not so confused by morphine. Let me check you out now, okay?"

Jay agreeably fell back in bed, and I began to examine him. His skin was damp and cool, a sick, neutral shade. His bony arms were braided with the knots and clots of old needle-track markings. A blue swastika tattoo adorned one shoulder. The right side of his chest sounded tympanitic against my finger percussion, an indication that his lung remained collapsed.

When I finished listening and looking and touching, I felt strangely empty-handed. As though my entire investigation had yielded little evidence of a human life. I looked into Jay's dark chestnut eyes and sadly wondered why they required so much dulling, why his very existence begged for constant anesthetic. I began to feel sorrow for Jay's unlived life.

I had to nudge him awake again. "Jay, the notes in your chart indicate that you don't want a chest tube to reexpand your lung. Or a blood transfusion to give your body more oxygen. But you still want full CPR. Why is that?" I asked.

Bleary-eyed, he responded, "Well, doc, I don't believe in taking other peoples' blood—it's against my religion. And the other doctor said the chest tube would hurt. Shit, and I mean, like, why wouldn't I want people to try to save me if I'm dying?" he asked in a tone conveying superior sensibility.

"But, Jay, don't you think that your position is contradictory?"

"No, I don't," he replied, indignant. "It's completely noncontradictory with the ways I feel and believe."

"No, what I mean," I tried to explain, "is that it seems pointless to want CPR if you don't want transfusions and lab work and medications and chest tubes."

"Well, that's what I want," he said. "There ain't no contradictions in that."

I felt myself wanting to break free of my physician's decorum and scream in utter frustration. Although resolute about fully disclosing medical facts to patients, I wasn't always certain about the propriety of revealing my personal feelings—particularly if they might challenge a patient's religious beliefs.

I resolved that Jay and I did have an odd but intimate personal relationship of sorts. After all, I had absorbed the sounds of his lungs through my ears, held his sweaty head within my hands while he vomited a beef burrito, palpated the interior of his fissured rectum with my finger, painstakingly monitored the beatings of his heart, unwillingly breathed into my own lungs the alcohol from his rancid breath, and carried him home inside my head many nights. I had listened attentively to the story of his life, often fabricated and always evolving.

So I decided to speak to Jay in a personal voice. "Jay," I said, shaking my head, "I just have to say that you're completely nuts, absolutely bananas, with this CPR thing."

He looked directly at me. Surprised. Brows furrowed. Listening.

I continued, "It's like taking your Mustang to the body shop when, at the same time, you've decided against giving it gasoline and an engine. I mean, we can bang on your body with CPR while you're dying, if that's what you want. But your body won't run without blood and lungs. CPR is a painful way to die under the circumstances."

Jay laughed and clutched his aching side again. "Pretty funny, doc. The car thing." After his paroxysms of pain subsided, he said he'd reassess his position.

"Fine," I said, "I'll return in a couple of hours to check in on you."

"Yeah," he weakly responded.

"By the way," I asked, genuinely interested, "when did you find religion? And what religion? You once told me that you didn't believe in any god, anything spiritual."

Jay turned toward the large window overlooking the courtyard on his right. After pausing briefly he said, "I found Jesus through my aunt. She's a Jehovah's Witness." He painstakingly withdrew a pamphlet from his bedside table and offered it to me. "Here, want to read this?"

The Watch Tower. I was very familiar with it. I could not imagine Jay at one of the congregation meetings. "No, no thanks."

"Shit, Doctor Scannell, it's like I found a reason for…" But then Jay began coughing and splinting his chest with his arms again. I suggested he refrain from speaking and told him that I really wanted to hear about his experience when he was better able to talk.

Walking down the hallway, I wondered about the story behind Jay's recent religious conversion. What I knew of him made me doubt that he could even sense a god or a heaven. He lived so close to the earth, at ground level, within a painfully narrow spectrum of life, personal experience cut off at the neck by booze and drugs.

When I returned to his room hours later, Jay reported that he had decided to forgo CPR. He also said that his breathlessness and his chest pain had become intolerable, and that he wanted a chest tube inserted for relief. "But no transfusions," he insisted. "And I need something for pain."

"Got it. No transfusions," I replied.

Jay's lung reexpanded with the tube, and, despite his protestations, we negotiated his narcotic intake downward. He was discharged two weeks later, but he bounced back to us within several days, emaciated, dehydrated, and so pale that his skin was translucent. His high fevers had returned. He asserted that he wanted only comfort care. Something for "pain all over my body," he said. On the second day of hospitalization, Jay's aunt informed him that he was no longer welcome to live in her basement; she said he was "too much trouble." This made Jay furious, and he denounced Jehovah. He ripped apart several copies of *The Watch Tower* and cast their remnants about his room.

Jay, now homeless and very fragile, remained with us while we waited for an available bed on the skilled-nursing facility. While we didn't think it possible, he became increasingly belligerent and hostile. He physically threatened several of us who refused his inordinate demands for narcotics and sedatives. Two social workers and one psychologist had no influence on his awful behavior. He remained oblivious to his damaging impact upon ward morale. His sole contemplative exercise consisted of scheming ways to procure drugs.

One pivotal day, I reached my critical limit of tolerance when informed of Jay's latest threat to yet another staff member. I rose from my office chair and almost ran, red-faced and jaw-clenched, to his bedside. There I yelled, "That's it, Jay! You're outa here!"

He appeared shocked, but only momentarily. Quickly he became defiant. "You can't kick me out," he proclaimed.

"Yes, I can!" I seethed. "You don't have a single treatable medical condition. This is an acute-care ward, not a MacDonald's where you can drop in when you like and order your favorite drugs. You're outa here! *Out!*"

"Well, I can't leave," he protested. "I don't have no place to go no more," he stated matter-of-factly.

"I don't care, Jay. That's no reason for hospitalization. Hundreds of homeless people would be here if it was. I mean it, Jay, you're out of here. Today. Now! You're one of the meanest, nastiest, most selfish people I've ever met. You've consistently treated everyone here like they're worthless. I have a duty to my staff and the other patients. They have a right to feel safe here, and your threats are over the line. And they've been that way for far too long. You're out!" I shouted, acutely aware of bounding pulsations in my neck and the piercing discomfort of my fingernails gouging my palms.

Storming out of his room, I suddenly felt afraid that Jay would retaliate somehow. He was so feral and lawless.

Still, I knew that my greater fear was the dreadful prospect of him remaining on the ward. Just within the prior week, he had threatened to kill one patient and had pushed a nurse against the wall while she administered an antibiotic to him.

Several paces beyond his doorway, I heard Jay wail like a faraway beast, "No!" and, "God, no!" over and over. The sounds he made were bloodcurdling, and they drew several patients from their rooms. Loud, grand sobbing ensued. But I continued to walk away from him. I decided that Jay could no longer manipulate me. That he would be made accountable for his behavior.

About an hour later, still distracted by our passionate interchange, I was summoned by Jay through Maggie, one of the nurses. I told her to inform him that I was busy, and that he should have been packed and out of the hospital by now. And that I could arrange for security to assist him should he need help leaving.

Soon after that, Maggie handed a note to me. "This is from your pen pal," she said.

The note read, "I'm sorry. Give me another chance."

I didn't believe him. Obviously, he thought he was dealing with someone naive.

Reluctantly, at the end of my workday, I returned to Jay's room. He was lying in bed, staring at the waffle-tiled ceiling. "What do you want, Jay?" I asked coldly.

Without looking at me he said, "I don't want to leave. I don't have no place to go."

"This is not about what *you* want or need," I declared. "This is about the other people here—patients and staff. You have no right to treat them the awful way that you do. And I am really, really tired of you lying to me. It's actually boring, Jay."

"Well, I'm in pain," he demurred as his chin puckered and reddened like a raspberry. His eyes began to churn out thin streams of tears.

"I'm sure you are," I calmly replied, resigning myself to the futility of discussing the reality of any life beyond his own.

During our ensuing silent showdown, I surveyed Jay's meager skeletal remains and thought again about the thin sliver of life in which he lived. He had had no substantial or lasting relationship with anyone: parents, siblings, wife, the army, friends, women, gods. His only consistent relationship was with pain.

Finally, I said, "Well, you can't stay here like this, Jay. You're making everyone's life miserable."

"I got no place to go," he replied.

"That's a misfortune of your own making," I responded. "You've somehow managed to antagonize anybody who has ever tried to help you. Everyone on the staff. It's your doing, Jay. No one here owes you a thing."

He started to whimper, and, for the first time, he looked scared. I wondered if it was just another act, a trick to manipulate me.

"Jay," I wearily began amid my uncertainty, "isn't there anyone or anything you have *ever* cared for besides yourself?"

He was quiet, staring at his clenched hands. They were pulling at the frayed edges of his green hospital blanket.

"No one? Ever?" I asked.

Silence.

"You know," I began, "I realize that life has been hard for you, but you…"

I fell speechless when Jay's sallow lips began to quiver. He shut his eyes violently, as though casting out visual demons.

But all he said, whispered, really, was "fish."

"Fish?" I asked, puzzled. "Who is Fish?" I racked my memory for a conversation we might have had about his pal Fish.

Jay wiped his runny nose against his blanket and, composing himself, said, "No. *Fishes.* You know, like little animals in water."

I envisioned Jay strolling the avenue with a sea bass in hand, tossing a football to an eager guppy in the park, attending cinema with a Pacific salmon. It was difficult for me to comprehend the possibility of meaningful relational experience with fish. Admittedly, I was handicapped in this matter, having lived life detached from the animal world. I had had no personal experience with pets and had exclusively viewed most animals as allergens. And yet I realized that in Jay's situation, a relationship of any nature, even with fish, was definitely preferable to having no relatedness to life at all.

Still, I thought, *fish?* They seemed so—cold. You couldn't pet them. Or walk them. You couldn't hold them or hug them without threatening their small lives. They heavily exuded attitude—a bored, aloof one; psychologically speaking, they were diagnosable avoidant personalities, should one even concede "personality" to them.

Then I thought, well, maybe, just maybe, these were the selling points for Jay. I could imagine him staring, inebriated, for hours at his brightly colored fish. They could entertain him with life safely contained behind glass walls. Not *too much* life, but life nonetheless, confined and manageable.

"Do you own fish?" I asked.

"I always did before," he answered softly. "Even when I was a kid. I ain't been able to keep none since I had to move around. When they kicked me out of my apartment I traded my tank—for whiskey, some heroin, stuff like that."

I pictured little Goldie—squirming, panic-stricken—on the bargaining table, accompanied by an angelfish and a couple of seahorses. Jay's enormous hands cupping around them, pushing them to the opposite side of the table as a pint of Jack Daniels is exchanged and wide-eyed Goldie's terror is caught in reflection by the glass bottle.

Even with his admission, I was excited and gratified that, perhaps, we finally identified something in the world to which Jay could export feelings of affection and attachment. I said, "Okay, Jay. You can stay here. But only if you stop threatening the nurses and patients. If you stop treating us like servants. Once more—and I mean only once more—and you're out."

He nodded.

Driving home that evening, I passed wide expanses of undeveloped land flanking the highway, rolling hills that seemed to flow uninterrupted into space. I imagined a ten-gallon fish tank, a 5-cc syringe, and a fifth of bad whiskey somewhere on that vast terrain, barely perceptible against the illimitable landscape, yet accommodating most of Jay's life.

The next day was a quiet one on the ward. Jay refrained from uttering a single threat or curse, at least audibly, to the staff. On morning rounds, he was dimmed and subdued, mindlessly watching television reruns.

"Hey, Jay," I greeted him.

"Hey," he responded without looking at me.

I watched a few minutes of *The Brady Bunch* alongside him. I wondered what Mrs. Brady would say if she were to discover that Mr. Brady had AIDS. When a commercial finally rescued me from the program, I asked Jay how things were going. He replied in monotone, "Yeah, things are fine."

I nodded, pushed myself off the chair, listened to his chest, and left his room after a few cursory exchanges between us.

Jay's emotional flatness persisted for many days. He rigidly confined himself to his corner room. He stopped pestering staff for drugs. He became wooden and laconic.

While Jay's previous conduct had been obnoxious and undesirable, his new muted demeanor disturbed me greatly. Increasingly, I experienced his spiritlessness as distressing and intolerable. I found myself desperately wanting him to show signs of life again.

One day I completed ward rounds early and signed out of the hospital at two in the afternoon. The sun was celebrating itself. In the parking lot, I opened the door to my subcompact car as a waft of deadening heat rushed out and ambushed me. I repeated my usual mantra for this occasion: "The next time, buy a light-colored car with air-conditioning."

After airing out the car, I drove to the local shopping mall. Though not entirely conscious of my motives, I had decided to purchase a small tank of fish—a bowl of life—for Jay.

I entered the eclectic drugstore near the toy shop and asked the clerk if his store carried fish. I discovered that the teenaged salesperson was new to the store. And to the English language. And to fish.

In telegraphic speech and hand signals I indicated that I wanted to buy a little bowl of fish that could fit on someone's nightstand. I drew the silhouette of a Pepperidge Farm fish cracker on a piece of newspaper. The young man finally understood. He directed me to three tanks of fish situated alongside plastic ukeleles and designer flyswatters at the rear of the store. He stood by idly as I began to select fish from the tanks. He knew nothing of fish taxonomy, and he declined to guess the number of fish that might live comfortably within one bowl.

So I chose fish on the basis of their colors, selecting the brightest life forms for Jay. I assumed the six that I picked were compatible with one another, even though I selected them from separate tanks. After some hesitation, I finally purchased one glass bowl and furnished it with plastic palm trees to suggest a tropical atmosphere. With relief, I found a compelling and unambiguously labeled product, "Best Fish Food," and I included that in my purchases.

I positioned the bowl of fish on the floor of my car, on the passenger's side, wedging it solidly against the seat with my tennis shoes and a box of Kleenex. Then I remembered that I had a print in my trunk that I had been lugging around for months; I decided to return to the mall and drop it off at the frame shop.

I quickly selected a compatible frame and brought it to the counter. The proprietor said it would be ready in twenty minutes, so I decided to wander through the mall while I waited.

But I got lost among the leprechauns. Giant four-leaved clovers. Pots o' gold centerpieces. The exuberant display of St. Patrick's Day paraphernalia in the jumbo Hallmark store. I lost track of time in the emerald aisles.

About an hour later, I returned to my car, one arm struggling with a shopping bag teaming with Irish tchotchkes and the other trying to prevent a large wooden frame from dragging against the cement parking lot.

I loaded my treasures into the trunk and entered the sauna that was my car. The little fish seemed unusually peaceful. I drove back toward the hospital along curving roads with great care, trying not to rock the fish bowl. At the first stoplight, I glanced down. One fish was floating atop the water. I thought its position was odd, but I wondered if it might be a normal sleeping posture for fish.

At the next light, startled by an errant driver, I jerked my car to a halt in the road. Two blocks later, back in the hospital parking lot, I immediately opened my car door for air. After enjoying a few deep, reviving breaths, I turned my sweaty head to glance at the fish bowl. Then a few seconds of slower-motioned time elapsed before I realized the horror—three of my little orange and golden fish were truant from the bowl. Hurriedly, I located one inside my tennis shoe and two others on the steamy black plastic floor mat. I was frantic, scooping them up with my bare hands, tossing them back into their half-filled, half-emptied bowl.

Steadying myself, I surveyed the fish again. Now three were floating motionless on the water's surface. The three remaining underwater appeared stunned, although I questioned my qualifications to interpret the nuances of their facial expressions.

I carried the fish bowl onto the ward and showed it to Maggie. She informed me that the floaters were actually dead, and that the other three were atypically placid. She tested the water with her finger and asked why it was so "blazing hot."

"Maybe I left it in my car too long?" I suggested.

"On a hot day like this? You're a murderess!" she exclaimed.

I told her what had happened at the mall and on the street. We stared at my sad community of fish, traumatized by multiple deaths, tsunamis, and heat waves. I thought I couldn't possibly offer these battered lives to Jay.

"You know," Maggie said, "they usually put them inside little baggies for you at the store. So they don't spill out of the water in your car."

I was learning a lot about a topic I had placed somewhere at the bottom of my list of things to study should I ever become bored.

"What do you think I should do now?" I asked.

"Well, what are they for?" she replied.

"They're for Jay," I answered. "He's so isolated. I think fish are the only things he relates to."

"Why? He enjoys pulling off their fins? Feeding them to sharks?" she asked.

Indeed, Jay had made a poor impression on the staff. "No," I replied, "he genuinely seems to like them. But maybe you're right, and maybe I'm being manipulated again. Though, you know, he couldn't possibly hurt these fish intentionally any more than I have done unintentionally."

"That's true," Maggie concurred. "Well," she said, "the little yellow one looks like she might need CPR. And the dazed one by the palm tree could use a battery, I think."

I felt defeated. "Do you think I could revive them with cold water?" I asked.

"Well, it might help the three still under water," she answered. "The three on top only require holy water now."

I took the fish to the bathroom and dropped the three rubbery floaters into the drain. I added cool, fresh tap water to the fish bowl and righted the palm trees which had been toppled in the havoc. The three remaining fish seemed oblivious to the deaths and the ruined landscape. They appeared unconcerned. They were ready to meet Jay.

Transporting the fish through the hallway, I explained to curious staff every few feet along the route that the fish were a gift for someone on the ward. From their responses, I surmised that the world was neatly divided into people like me whose souls didn't quite resonate with the spirit of the fish world and those for whom it did.

Finally in Jay's room, I set the bowl on the nightstand, making room for it among motorcycle magazines and crumpled wads of potato chip bags. Jay heard me disturb the cellophane, and he awoke.

"Hey, Jay, what do you think?" I asked, pointing to the fish.

He looked surprised, and his eyes showed a spark of life for the first time in many days. "Are those for me?" he asked, the enthusiasm of his voice sounding like a young boy's.

"Yes," I replied. "I know it's not the same as a big aquarium, but I thought you might enjoy them."

He glanced at the fish and smiled his half-toothless grin. "Thanks, doc. I do," he said. He began to stare at them intensely, just as I began to stare at him. He looked so weak and pale, and his skin was bloated like that of a drowned body washed to shore.

He was barely able to sit up. Before leaving, I moved the bowl closer to the edge of the nightstand so that he might see it better from the flat of his bed.

The next few days proved grim. Jay experienced terrible nerve pain, and he developed air hunger, gasping for oxygen. His blood pressure barely facilitated a flow of his thin blood throughout his body. He wanted only morphine and, sometimes, oxygen. He occasionally roused for lime jello or a sip of vanilla Ensure, and he would then gaze at the fish.

One such day, en route to Jay's room, Maggie informed me that the head nurse had announced during morning staff conference that she intended to enforce a hospital policy prohibiting pets in patients' rooms; and she had specifically advised the ward nurses to abstain from "getting involved" with Jay's fish.

I thanked Maggie for her warning and remarked that I was surprised and touched by the head nurse's concern. But, I said reassuringly, I thought the chances of a nurse becoming emotionally involved with the fish were rather remote.

Maggie guffawed. "Ah! That's great! You're not serious, are you?"

She placed her hand over her mouth when she realized I was earnest. "Oh, Kate," she said, "what she meant was that she didn't think we should be spending valuable nursing time caring for the fish. You know—feeding them, cleaning their bowl, changing the water."

"Oh," I replied. Then, "I didn't know you had to change the water."

"God, I'm glad it's humans you take care of," she laughed. She explained, "So now you'll have to learn how to attend fish, because Jay is too weak to care for them." She told me how I should transfer the fish to a holding tank while cleaning their bowl and changing their water, and she reminded me to feed them at intervals.

When I entered Jay's room, I noticed the fish bowl water was rather cloudy. The fish, however, appeared to be their usual aloof selves. They seemed unaffected by the haze, not colliding with one another, bumping against the palm trees, or thudding against the glass. Still, I resigned myself to the task and decided to take them to the bathroom for their ablutions. But I nearly dropped the fish bowl when Jay yelled, "No!"

"Oh, Jay," I shuddered, weak-kneed, "you scared the hell outa me!"

"Please don't take them," he whispered.

"Jay, I'm not removing them. I'm just going to clean their bowl."

"Do it here. Please," he begged.

So I filled an emesis basin with tap water and placed it on the window sill. I formed a net with packing gauze and, after some practice, captured the fish and transferred them to the basin. I washed brown and gray particles off the palm tree, and I removed a sticky layer of—what?—from the sides of the bowl. I filled the bowl with fresh water and returned the fish to their homestead. The fish remained poker-faced throughout.

Jay said that he only wanted to watch his fish a while. I asked if I could watch them with him. He nodded.

I sat in the chair near him and began to stare at the fish. I wondered how they could look so luminous, as though they harbored candles inside their bellies. They floated and drifted and slid through the water like golden ribbons unfurling. After a while, I realized I had been trying, unsuccessfully, to predict their movements and directions. But soon I was carried on their backs, unfurling with them, floating with them, relinquishing to unpredictable currents. Sailing through a great, immense sea indifferent to my presence. I felt peaceful.

Some time later—how long?—my attention snapped back to the room, and I looked at Jay. I watched his

brown eyes roving back and forth following the fish until
he fell asleep.

Over the next few days, Jay became increasingly som-
nolent. I spent my time with him by sitting nearby, listening
to him breathe, and studying his fish. Once, he awoke to
discover me in his bedside chair, mesmerized by the fish. I
had been staring a while, trying to recall a melody invoked
by their swoops and trails through the water. He smiled at
me and said, "You get it now, don't you?"

I returned his smile, a little embarrassed. It dawned on
me that he was aware of sharing something with me. That
he was even advising me about my experience. "Yeah, I
think I do," I replied. "In fact, I'm going to miss your little
fish this weekend."

"Well," he offered, "if you do, you can just close your
eyes and see them. When you understand about fishes you
can do that."

I tried not to cry. But a chaos of emotions flooded me
with this mystery breaking open. Suddenly I felt swept
into a great sea with Jay, one that was carrying us to new
territory. I could barely stand him looking at me, smiling
so luminously.

I composed myself and asked him if there were anything he envisioned needing for the weekend, as the
on-call physicians the next three days would be unfamiliar
with his case.

"No," he replied. And then, uncharacteristically, he
said, "Have a great weekend, doc."

I had never heard Jay wish good tidings to anyone
before. I replied, stunned, "Thanks, Jay. Thanks. I will." I
put my hand on his arm and said good-bye . He was still
smiling directly at me, and it felt as though he might never
stop.

The weekend proved to be exceptionally hot and humid. I spent much of my time cataloging entries from medical journals into my AIDS notebooks. On Sunday morning, feeling restless, I was surprised to find myself with the urge to walk through the redwoods near my home. This was a foreign impulse for me. Although the forest was only six or seven blocks from my house, I had lived a stranger alongside it for years.

I drove to the redwoods in my sauna-on-wheels, checking several times along the way to verify that my car's heater was indeed turned off. Sticky sweat drenched me by the time I arrived at the moss-covered rocks outlining the parking lot along Skyline Drive.

Once out of the car, it was a sweet relief to feel the air pry the damp shirt off my back and chest. I entered a path that promised shade. Its floor was covered with soft spongy cedar needles and sticky brown clumps of—what? The sun was shape-shifting patterns through the boughs of giant trees that, I thought, seemed the heights of great prayers or poems. There were sounds that at first seemed to be one single sound; then they unraveled into separate threads: a moaning eucalyptus bark, a starling's song, leaves crackling underfoot, chattering long grass.

My lungs expanded along the walk, and I could feel my feet spread out to more fully meet the ground. A shaft of sunlight blinded me. A small puddle of forest water sucked at my shoe. A swarm of gnats formed a net across my face.

I began to feel rooted and green and alive and connected to the woods. I imagined my fingers fanning outward like a hand of fern leaves, my brown hair tossed by the breeze like a field of wheat grass, my legs as strong as the muscular trunk of a sturdy redwood.

I arrived at a clearing. A toppled redwood lay near a cliff that overlooked the San Francisco Bay, inviting me to sit.

From this vista I tried to locate my home, but I was too turned around by the twists and turns and swoops of the trails that had carried me there. I found a nook in the tree trunk that supported my back, and I sat staring at the bay. After some time, I closed my eyes to this great beauty and imagined, instead, the small fish in Jay's room. I began to follow them in their unpredictable swoops through the water. Looping and gliding and turning.

Then I remembered how desperate I had been for Jay to be inside life. And I realized how, in bringing him fish, I had been compelled by impulses that I trusted but did not fully understand. I had insisted upon Jay belonging to this world, being claimed by it. I thought of how my own sense of belonging was expanding, too, through a succession of patients' lives inviting me into the world, day to day, on the AIDS ward. And how it was also more than that—it was the very trees around my home, the sounds of the forest, the breakers in the bay, the fish. I wanted Jay to know this before he died.

On Monday morning, Maggie warned me that Jay was dying. I went to his room and found him barely alive, with his jaw hung open and his limbs in random arrangement across the bed. The fish bowl had been moved to the opposite edge of his nightstand, near the window, beyond his view. The three fish were belly up in their heated glass pool full of stone-gray water. I placed Jay's wiry arms close to his body, and I straightened his legs. A foul odor wafted from his mouth.

Stroking his forehead, I felt tremendous sadness and a deep sense of peace all at once. I thought about the trees on my walk, how some were bent and twisted and broken, diseased or decaying, and others were straight and intact, vigorous and healthy.

I was angry about the carelessness with which our fish had been placed in the ruinous heat of the burning sun, certainly the cause of their demise. I took the tepid bowl in my hands, anticipating another funeral march to the bathroom. But, as I rounded the corner of Jay's bed, he exclaimed, "No!"

His voice startled me, and I transmitted my shock to the fish which then began to bob in the turbulent, murky water. "Oh, Jay," I managed, unnerved, "you're awake!"

"Please don't take the fishes," he pleaded, barely audible.

"Uhh…" I deliberated, trying to decide how I might best break the news of our fishes' deaths. Looking into the bowl, I noticed that one fish had developed ill-defined, fuzzy edges, blurring through a semisolid state that gradually blended into the watery medium. A terrible stench rose from the bowl.

I returned to Jay's bedside and replaced the bowl on his nightstand. "God, Jay," I reluctantly began, "you know, I really hate to tell you this, but the fish…well, our fishes, died. I'm so sorry."

Slowly, he turned his half-mast eyes to me and replied, "Yeah, I know that."

I was stunned. My mind somersaulted through my usual ways of deciphering the people around me, and it landed inside a black hole. All I could say moments later was, "You *know* they're dead?"

Jay closed his eyes and smiled faintly to convey affirmation.

"Hmm, and…you still want them here?" I asked.

He nodded.

"Oh, Jay, I could bring new fishes, and we could place a sign here telling people to keep them from the window. Even put a sunshade around them."

But Jay shook his head. "I want them. Our fishes. I like to watch them float."

I looked to the sad flotilla, then back to Jay. I began to feel my black hole filling up, the four floating bodies inside the room drifting into it. I told him that I understood and left shortly thereafter.

In the hallway, Edna, the head nurse, approached me. She informed me that I would have to remove Jay's fish. There was, indeed, a hospital policy prohibiting pets on the ward.

Yet I knew that the fish must stay. In a flash of self-congratulatory brilliance I rejoined, "But they're not pets. They're *dead*."

"Dr. Scannell," Edna reproached, "the policy doesn't distinguish between living and dead pets!"

"Edna," I explained, "these are *fish*. And they're in a *bowl*. The spirit of the policy surely pertains to unmanageable animal behavior. Not only are these creatures confined to a tiny bowl, but they're also *dead*."

She responded, "Again, doctor, the policy doesn't distinguish 'pets' by type or by degree of liveliness. Those fish must be removed from Jay's room."

But I was determined. I replied, "Edna, our cafeteria serves dead fish to patients on this ward every day. By that precedent, there can't be a prohibition against Jay's dead fish."

"Oh, I give up," she said. As she turned away she sounded exasperated, and she mumbled, "I'll take your arguments to the staff meeting."

Later that day, I returned to Jay's room to change the nearly opaque water in the fish bowl. As I transferred our lifeless fish to the holding basin, one fell apart like flaky pie crust. I tried to force it back into a fish shape when I returned it to its bowl, but it looked more like a crude madeleine. I positioned the bowl to the side of the night-stand in Jay's view. I discarded the shaker of fish food into the wastebasket.

Over the next few days, I would round with Jay and the fish, each of us just seeming to float in a great sea that held us all somewhere together. I would close my eyes and recall my swoops and twists along the forest paths, the view of the bay from the felled redwood in the park, the tapestry of sound in the forest. I remembered the way I unfurled with the goldfish, my experience of being carried by unmarked currents. I mostly remembered Jay the way he looked when he had smiled at me and said, "You get it now, don't you?"

And Jay died like this, floating alongside our fishes. To this day, I can close my eyes and see them moving through the space between us.

Death Etiquette

Summoned or not, the god will come.
—Motto over the door of Carl Jung's house.

When Elton began to dement, I told him that it might help if he wrote down the things he wanted to remember. I bought him a spiral notebook and a dozen Bic pens.

He became quite the scribe. He insisted on committing to paper *everything* anyone said to him. When I rounded with him each morning, he'd not allow a word between us to escape his record. And he'd have to register the date, the time of day, and my name as a heading with our every encounter. I could have been visiting him one hour before, and still he'd insist on writing a new heading for our interaction.

Elton's obsession with documentation became increasingly problematic over time as his AIDS dementia advanced and his ability to process information progressively faltered. Conversations with him became laborious, even tortuous. The glacial pace of his transcription was maddening. He generally managed a string of three or four words at one time. Sometimes he'd get stuck on a word and rewrite it repeatedly before connecting with the next one. Occasionally, he would simply stop at the end of a page, where he'd remain suspended, as though he had traveled a path to a cliff's edge; if you flipped his notebook to the next sheet, he would resume his writing.

I began to speak with Elton in spartan, telegraphic phrases. I'd often sound like Tarzan. "You—pain?" I would ask. Or, pointing to his stomach, "Good today?"

Elton was born in Oklahoma, and he spoke naturally with a slow drawl and a gentle bend to his words. One late effect of his dementia, as though he had also forgotten his drawl, was a subtle shortening of his rubbery vowels, shrinking his a's and his o's toward a more Midwestern pronunciation.

One morning I asked him my usual question. "You—okay?"

He looked up from his buckwheat pancakes with maple syrup and replied simply, "Doctor, how am I supposed to die?"

He was staring at me with an overly intense expression that on someone else might have appeared as caricaturized earnestness. But I knew Elton was incapable of insincerity; he had shed self-conscious reflection and forgotten small pretensions during the last months of his dementia. I felt his expression setting permanently into my memory: his wrinkled and pocked forehead, his prematurely grayed mustache, his furrowed, contorted brow, his thin mouth raised at one corner. His blue, watery eyes looked so trustfully at me.

Elton and I had shared many conversations regarding his illness and approaching death, and I had always been forthright with him. But I doubted now that it was possible to have a complex discussion of death through the barriers of Elton's dementia; it seemed fated for disjointed fragmentation through its piecemeal processing into

Elton's notebook. I imagined our conversation ultimately lying across his notepaper like disorderly heaps of splintered Lincoln logs—dangling participles and split infinitives and sentence fragments—only vaguely suggesting the larger construct. Also, I was anxious about the time it would require for Elton to filter such a complicated discussion through the excruciatingly tedious pace of his handwriting.

Elton's question was timely. His multiple infections were whittling him away, critically reducing the balance of his life. Although I had become relatively comfortable with the frequency of death in my work, I still found it painful to confirm its reality with individual people.

Besides, there he was, looking at me like that.

So I resigned myself to the long haul ahead. I plopped myself down on the bed next to Elton and instructed myself to simply drop into the slow warp of time in which he lived. I regretted having drunk so much coffee that morning.

Preparing to speak, I noticed that Elton did not reach for his notebook. I felt greatly relieved. However, within seconds, I was overcome by terrible guilt. He's even forgetting his notebook now, I sadly reflected.

"Elton—notebook?" I reminded him.

"No. Just want to talk," he responded.

"Okay," I replied, relieved again.

I looked squarely at him, centering my eyes on his, and girded myself. I began slowly: "Elton, it's likely that you'll die because your lungs will fail to get enough oxygen to your body, or your heart will stop pumping your blood. One of your many infections, or even a new one, will probably tip you toward your death." I then explained how his wasting and dementia threatened his physical survival. How his "MAI" and "CMV" infections spelled trouble for his bowel and vision, respectively. I spoke carefully, in short sentences and leisurely cadence, watching Elton's face to monitor his comprehension. Throughout, he remained silent, nodding several times as though pondering my words.

Finally, finally, finally, I finished. I did it! I silently congratulated myself.

But then Elton wrinkled his nose and grimaced. He looked quite disturbed. He said, "No, I mean, how am I *supposed* to die? What should I *do?*"

I felt foolish. Apparently, I had been speaking at length for no reason. My only consolation came from the fact that my long and obviously superfluous soliloquy had not needed Elton's recording. I looked again into his incredibly sincere face.

"Elton," I replied, "I'm not sure what you mean. Are you asking me about wills? Or funeral preparations? Stuff like that?"

He answered, "No, no, not that."

"Oh, you mean how do you accept death? Or have a sense of God?"

"Nope," he replied, disconcerted and shaking his head.

"Well, I promise you that I'll do everything I can to keep you comfortable. Is that what you mean by how you'll die?"

His expression turned to one of complete frustration, and he looked away for a moment. Then he turned to me and said, "No. I want to know what I should be *doing* while I'm dying."

I was stunned, finally hearing Elton's inquiry as a simple question about a point of etiquette. "You mean," I asked, incredulous, "you want to know how you should behave? If there are proper manners you should follow, maybe?"

"Yes," he replied matter-of-factly, his face finally relaxing. "Yes, doctor, that's what I want to know," he said calmly.

I was stymied. People had always spoken about the "manner of death" in which human life passes, but I had never before heard the phrase taken so literally. Despite the hundreds of bedside discussions in which I had participated, I had neither heard nor considered Elton's question before; no one had ever raised the issue of a formal protocol or proper etiquette at death. While Elton's question initially sounded naive and rather besides the point, it also seemed to be such an instinctive and natural inquiry that I was surprised to be hearing it for the first time.

"Oh, Elton," I began, "there is nothing that you need to do. And there's nothing that you're expected to do. You don't have to be polite or perform for anybody."

"But it seems important," he insisted.

"Death?" I asked.

"Yeah. It seems like I should be doing something special when it happens," he explained.

I was afraid that I wouldn't be able to soothe Elton's distress by answering his question satisfactorily. On a much lesser scale, his quandary reminded me of the time, decades earlier, when my father took me to a local parade honoring Denny McLain of the Detroit Tigers. As Denny drove past us, waving from the back of a red Ford convertible, my father looked down at me and pronounced, "This is important, Kate." Then he looked away, back toward the parade. I didn't understand my father's grave announcement, but he seemed to be inferring that I needed to do something to respect the significance of the occasion. So I cried. My father turned to me again, and just stared, a completely befuddled expression on his face.

"Well, I know what you mean about feeling like everyone else except you knows the right way to be," I said. "Like there's a big secret about the right way to live and the right way to die, and everyone decided not to let you in on it."

"Yeah, that's how it seems," he said.

"Elton," I began, "most people I know feel that way, too. But the truth is that there is no one great secret."

"Think so?" he asked, pursing his lips and merging his eyebrows.

"Yes, I'm sure. There is no correct 'manner' of death. And it's no time to take up acting lessons. You can die any way you want to."

He nodded.

"Elton," I asked, "do you know how you want to die?"

"Well," he said, "I believe what you said. I really do. But fact is that I've never thought about dying before."

"So?"

"Well, doc," he hesitated, "I still want something to do when it happens. I'd like to have something I can do."

I hadn't been aware of behaving or speaking as a physician with Elton through most of our conversation; the majority of our communication had seemed nonmedical. But now I understood that my being a physician meant something to Elton—it was important. He was suffering, and as his physician, I was being asked to tend to that suffering, his question.

"Well," I said, "I guess you don't have to worry ahead of time, because when death comes it tells you what to do.

I think it takes you and leads you, like on a dance floor, and then you know exactly how to follow it when it takes you in its arms."

He looked less uncertain. Then he drawled, "Yeah, follow."

"Elton," I continued, "when the time comes, you'll have something to do; you'll follow, and you'll know exactly how. And you'll feel absolutely fine doing it. I'm sure of this."

He sat quietly for a few moments before smiling softly and replying, "Okay, thanks, doc. That's all I wanted to know. Like a dance..." He returned with great appetite to his buckwheat pancakes.

As I rose from his bed and walked away, I imagined congregations of sack-clothed monks preparing their entire lives for the moment of death. Of heavily robed nuns secluded for decades within a dark cloister, premeditating their afterlives. I thought about my own preoccupation with death, the way it accompanied me in daily thought and meditation.

And then there was Elton for whom death would appear suddenly, as a stranger. I envisioned it whisking him off his feet like an emboldened dance partner in the final moments of his life. I prayed that it would be gentle with him. Tender and patient.

I also hoped that Elton would have time to talk with his partner a while, enough to get to know him a little.

Most of all, I hoped that Elton would find himself swept away by the dance itself, throwing in a few of his own steps, his unique movements, and finding the great secret that belonged only to him. It seemed important.

Loving Someone to Death

Love gets its name (amor) from the word for
hook (amus) which means to capture or be captured.
—Andreas Capellanus, The Art of Courtly Love

If I could wash one memory from my physician's hands, it would be of Eric. Even now, years later, as I think of him, I fold my hands reflexively into a tight fist, as though trying to wring out the imprint of his life left in my palm. His visage still intrudes during sleepless nights.

What I first remember is his swollen, moon-shaped head, so puffed with fluid and air as to obscure the natural landscape of a human face; two dark pinholes marking the usual location of eyes; and his eerie smile, seemingly detached from the reality of his awful physical predicament, floating like a loose rose petal over his spongy chin.

His relentless crescent smile had sent chills down my spine. It rarely budged during his prolonged torture in his hospital bed. It did not waver when yet another plastic tube or surgical incision split his fragile skin wide open like tumescent fruit. It remained steadfast when the soft substance of his heels and buttocks partially decomposed into rancid slurries of bedsores. It remained rigidly fixed while his mother, Mrs. Green, regularly discharged her venomous anger around his bedside.

I experienced profound dread the moment I walked into the lives of these two people. As my foot crossed the threshold of Eric's doorway, I felt as though I had stepped into something horrid and thick and sticky.

Eric lay restrained in bed, looking like a dim-witted, pathetic soul trapped within an expansive and complicated web. Monitoring lines and cables and colorful wires and plastic tubes emanated like fibers from sundry attachment sites on his body and tethered him to far reaches of his room: to intravenous fluid bottles, antibiotic pouches, cardiac monitors, ventilators, urine bags, chest-tube suction devices. And, most centrally, to his mother.

"Well, I have been waiting for you," seethed his mother. "I've had to fight with everyone here for almost three weeks just to obtain decent care for my son. And I understand that *you're* the director of this ward?"

Her bitter, angry voice landed on my ear drums as a caustic dare, on my body as a hostile shove. Minutes earlier, having returned to work from a restful vacation, I had been cautioned by the receptionist that "the witch mother" was lying in wait for me inside Eric's room. A frustrated staff nurse had greeted me at the entryway and found herself speechless when trying to prepare me for Mrs. Green. The charge nurse had interrupted us to inform me that staff requested conference time with me later that day to discuss the "problem" of Eric and his mother.

These warnings hung from my neck like a lead yoke when I encountered Eric's mother. In her presence, as the AIDS ward director, I felt like an accidental prisoner of her uncertain war. A happenstance in her crosshairs, her unfocused jittery aim issuing from a place of interior darkness where time was not wasted on discriminating targets. Where there was a kind of desperation to find an enemy.

She was an imposing and ominous figure who appeared to become even taller as time passed. She staked out a broad territory around Eric's hospital bed, and the ICU nurses, scurrying about with their tasks, seemed to bounce off her vast force field. I imagined her to have huge, suffocating, dark wings that could overfill the room and practiced talons poised for a kill. Her face was calloused and irregularly angular, like a compact mass of old stones. She looked at me through the dark incisions between her eyelids. She made me feel small and afraid and insecure. Her hatred and enmity insinuated themselves through the cracks in my self-defenses. She fanned an awful throbbing unrest somewhere within my unconscious. Confused and off center, I wondered frantically how this stranger could affect me so deeply. Why I felt as though I might be consumed by her.

I had trouble locating my voice, but, eventually, I managed to say, "Mrs. Green, I'm Doctor Scannell. What I'd like to do is familiarize myself with your son's case and examine him. If you can give me fifteen minutes or so, I'd be in a better position to understand and discuss his care with you. Will that be all right?"

A moment of silence ensued during which it seemed she was plotting a strategy. She slowly folded her fierce wings against her chest and snapped her head to the side, fixating me with one dark eye.

"I will be here," she replied, dramatic pauses between each word.

I walked to the attendant nurse's desk, and, with Mrs. Green's stare boring into the back of my neck, opened Eric's medical chart and began to review the treating physicians' daily progress notes from the previous weeks. The entries revealed only limited medical details of Eric's case and even less personal information about Eric. Rather, the notes focused heavily upon the day-to-day moods of his mother and the status of her litigious threats against the hospital and its medical staff. Eric was virtually spectral. His medical condition was daily and summarily noted as "poor prognosis," and the routine plan of management was to "continue supportive care."

Eric was a thirty-one-year-old man who, three months before admission, had been diagnosed with AIDS. His diagnostic features were dementia and extensive Kaposi's sarcoma, a cancerlike tumor of the skin that had rarely been seen before the AIDS epidemic.

On admission, Eric was laboring for air, and he was diagnosed quickly with pneumonia. Nonetheless, after three days of antibiotics, he developed respiratory failure and, at his mother's insistence, he was intubated: that is, one end of a breathing tube was threaded through his nostril and into his windpipe, and the other end was connected to a respirator.

Within days, Eric recovered sufficiently to warrant removal of his breathing tube and detachment from the respirator. However, six days later, he once again became desperately ill, and his chest X-ray revealed a new pneumonia. Aggressive, broad-spectrum antibiotic therapies were given to treat this infection. Eric also received a series of blood transfusions through intravenous lines and daily infusions of canned nutrition through a feeding tube channeled into his stomach via his nostril. The chart entries reported that Mrs. Green had stood steadfast at her son's bedside, constantly directing the staff to "do something" as her son's respiratory status faltered again and again.

The treating physicians had counseled Mrs. Green against reintubating her son, an intervention they considered inhumane and futile. But she had been successful in persuading them otherwise. Eric's breathing, his very life, again became dependent upon the respirator.

A week later his left lung collapsed as a result of the excessive air pressures generated by forceful respirator breaths. Mrs. Green then insisted that a chest tube be inserted through Eric's rib cage to decompress his collapsed lung. That evening, a stiff plastic tube was pushed through an incision in Eric's chest, between two of his left ribs. During the procedure, some air leaked and tracked through spaces between the skin and muscles surrounding his trunk, inflating his face and previously emaciated body into hideous, swollen proportions. He lay in bed like a grotesque monster zeppelin, with multiple needles puncturing the tenuous surface of his body, his smile unwavering.

At the desk, I finally closed Eric's chart, feeling a bilious swill rushing into my throat. What horrific theater was this? How could this barbaric situation have arisen? Who could have conceived such a nightmare for this terminally ill, demented man? It was torture, pure and simple. It was a level of cruelty evoking surrealism.

My first wish was to be made invisible and escape the macabre scene in Eric's room. A mere twenty minutes earlier my life had had nothing to do with this insanity; I was maneuvering my Dodge Colt through the morning traffic on 580, hot coffee in my traveling mug and Anita Baker on the tape deck. I was actually looking forward to going to work. Now I fantasized having driven beyond the hospital exit, to the San Leandro marina. I wanted to go back in time and redo the morning.

My meandering was stopped short by Mrs. Green's acidic voice. "And?" she said, bending that one word across several deflections. After exchanging tense looks with the nurse, I turned in my chair to face Mrs. Green. Her legs and arms were severely crossed. Raw anger burned from the surface of her face and infused the room with uncomfortable heat. My own face twitched between a smile and a cringe. The muscles between my shoulder blades knotted.

"Mrs. Green," I said, "Your son is very ill. I'm sure you know that, and…"

She rolled her eyes, stopping me momentarily.

I continued. "And I need to examine him now so I can make a better medical assessment."

She raised one weighty eyebrow and warned again, "Go ahead. I'll be right here."

As I laid my examining hand on Eric's body, I strove hard not to gag. My slightest touch on his mottled skin produced crepitus, a sound formed by compression of air pockets trapped within tissues, like the popping of bubbled cellophane packing material. The gruesome smell of his decaying flesh, putrid and intense, somewhere between life and death, sickened me. Puddles of his liquefying tissues formed yellow and green and red stains on the bed sheet under his buttocks and heels. His lips were bloodless and puffy, and thick brown crusts filled the musty cavern of his mouth like an old honeycomb. A watery ooze sweated off the surface of his water-bottle legs.

I wanted to take a machete to the lines and cables suspending Eric within this atrocity. I wanted to free him, pick him up, carry him in my arms to a safe place.

But there he lay with that disturbing, steadfast smile and no show of resistance. I tested to see if his smile might be artifact to a mechanical upward pull of his mouth created by the swelling in his face. But a gentle nudge of his lips revealed an easy downward displacement by my finger. Could he *really* be smiling? Consciously?

"Eric, Mr. Green," I said, "my name is Doctor Scannell, and I'll be taking over your medical care. You can't talk with that tube in your throat, but, if you can hear me, perhaps you can nod your head to answer some questions?"

I felt silly and self-conscious, because I did not really expect that Eric would respond. I assumed that no conscious being would have ever elected the circumstances of his situation. Also, Eric appeared like a disorganized heap of damaged body parts rather than a functionally integrated human with cognition and awareness. A cadaveric marionette attached to a web of tubes and lines, his mother yanking the strings.

But then Eric nodded yes.

I was shocked. I wondered if his nod were a reflex jerking of his neck muscles or a physical buck from the respirator.

I asked, "Eric, can you hear me?"

He nodded again.

"*Yes*, he can hear you," interrupted his mother. "*We* can hear you. We have done nothing but hear your colleagues for the last three weeks. We've heard everything they've said. And we're sick and tired of hearing their excuses and deceptions and sorry predictions. I'm tired of you all being *tired* about my son's chances. I've read about lots of people with AIDS who survived for years. I'll be damned if my son is going to die because this hospital doesn't think a poor man deserves expensive medical care. I'll have my lawyers and the press here in two seconds.

You think I'm kidding? You just ask the last doctors who were here. I know what bad medical treatment poor people get."

I thoroughly despised the moment. While I had weathered a variety of prejudices and projections that had been thrust upon me as a physician, this woman was exuding particularly virulent hostilities. I felt as though she had just defecated all over me. And though I understood that Mrs. Green's vitriol was primitive and impersonal, still I felt her trying to annihilate *me*. Intellectual comprehension did not prevent me from feeling small, afraid, and insecure.

I scrambled internally for protective cover, for a different way to understand what was happening. Quickly, I recognized that I was operating from a familiar territory: an old, childhood place of feeling anonymous, small, and invisible within my family of eleven siblings. Wishing I were elsewhere, on more developed and mature ground, identifying the territory of my experience at least allowed me to orient myself more precisely within the chaos at hand. To understand better how Mrs. Green's ability to annihilate me succeeded through her inability to recognize me, allow me an individual humanity.

And then, in slow motion, I glanced back at Eric, simultaneously realizing how completely Mrs. Green had annihilated her own son. Literally and figuratively, he was disappearing in the shadow of her great, towering presence, her archetypal form.

"I'm an important woman," she said, "and I know lots of people. I will not be dismissed."

"Mrs. Green," I said, "you and I have no bad business between us. I have no intention of…"

She interrupted me. "You people think that, just because my son is poor, he is not worth saving. You think he costs too much. Well, let me tell you, it will cost you much more in a big fat lawsuit than you ever..."

Her voice trailed off as I turned inward once again, trying to sort out this awful, broken mess. It seemed to me that Eric's life did not exist for Mrs. Green beyond the perimeter of her self-enclosed wall of mirrors. He was a mere accessory to her "mother's outfit" that she was forced to wear for the dramatic occasion of her son's death and dying.

Angry and frustrated, I reluctantly concluded that Mrs. Green's narcissism vastly outweighed the probability of making myself visible or understood and that my primary task was to bring Eric to center focus in the room. I counseled myself to step back from her. At close range and frozen in her stare was the exact position in which she wanted me. I needed to find a place inside myself where old territory didn't quake and demons didn't rule.

Luckily, something finally broke through the impossibility of the moment, like a footbridge spanning dark waters and revealed by the sudden lifting of fog. I became able to speak calmly and confidently with a sense of internal authority. "Mrs. Green," I said, "you don't know me. So I suggest that you try to start over. But I will *not* assume responsibility for your personal history with the rest of the world. So, how do you want it to be with us?"

I fantasized Eric applauding in the background, his voice harmonizing with mine; but his pillowy lips only maintained their strange smile. Mrs. Green recoiled and tried to stare me down, to pulverize me with her hatred. I felt my foothold loosening, the fog pulling me in again. My heart began to race.

Another nurse entered the room, clearly sidestepping Mrs. Green's stare. She was visibly upset, agitated. I thought she was going to cry. She exchanged an infusion bag and examined the skin sites around Eric's intravenous lines. She glanced at me as if to plead for something, and then she hurried away.

Mrs. Green finally spoke. "I will wait for you outside. When you're through here, *doctor*." She then exited through the door as though royal processional music were playing in the background.

The attendant nurse and I looked at each other like two fellow prisoners. I turned to Eric and said, "Eric, since you can hear me, I need to determine if you understand what's going on."

Eric nodded once up and once down.

"Doctor," said the nurse, "he really does seem to understand, at least simple questions."

I tried to contain my disbelief. "Eric, are you in pain?" I asked.

He shook his head no.

I looked again at the nurse, whose tented eyebrows and agape mouth mirrored my own. How could he *not* be in agony? Could he be so thoroughly demented that he didn't know he was suffering?

"Eric," I said, "you are very sick. Your body is giving up. You look like a pin cushion—all these needles and tubes sticking through your body. Don't they bother you?"

Again he shook his head no.

"Eric," I asked, "are you making the decisions about your care, all these needles and tubes, yourself?"

"No," he indicated.

"Well, is your mother making those decisions for you?"

He motioned "yes."

"Do you always agree with her decisions?"

"Yes," he nodded.

I was mystified. Numbed by the senselessness surrounding me. I fell silent. I sighed deeply. I sat on Eric's bed and held his doughy hand. I felt myself becoming calm, almost mindless. I looked around at the collarette of brightly colored infusion bags surrounding him like a cheap, gaudy choker: plastic bladders full of ruby-red blood, gilt-yellow urine, pearl-white nasogastric feedings, crystal-clear saline.

I placed my other hand on Eric's soft, spongy shoulder. I tried to look into his eyes, but they were completely submerged behind his engorged lids.

"Eric," I continued, "does your mother ask your advice about your care?"

His head did not move.

"Eric, sweetheart, I'm sorry but I really need to know if..."

Immediately, Eric's smile flattened and disappeared. So, too, did the tracing on his cardiac monitor. The nurse moaned, "Oh, god, no, not again," as the code blue siren sounded. Mrs. Green rushed toward the room, screaming, "Do something! Do something!" A team of nurses and respiratory therapists tried to maneuver beyond her obstructive presence in the doorway. She was shouting something about me, us, all trying to kill her son. She yelled, "How can you do this to me?"

I could not believe the thicket of anguish and dread around me. The uneasy silence of many coworkers who appeared to be there with knives against their throats. The dulled shock in the nurses' eyes, as though forced to bear witness to something unbearable.

As this barbaric ritual unfolded, I pleaded several times with Mrs. Green: "Please, I know it's hard, but let your son go in peace..."

"Murderer!" she screamed only. "Murderer! Do something! Do something!"

One nurse assisting with medications choked on her sobs while sorting out the tangles of intravenous tubes. A respiratory therapist kept silent, only shaking his head as if to say, "It's no use."

"You'd better not let my boy die!" wailed Mrs. Green.

I watched the gathering of coworkers swarming around Eric's body. Eyes fixed rigidly before them, forced to see; hands wanting to disown their own movements. I knew from reading Eric's medical chart that they had all been through this gruesome exercise with him once before.

Then the cardiac monitor beeped, registering a weak rhythm that grew into a sustaining cadence, rousing Eric from death once again.

A young nurse squeezed her eyes shut and covered her face with her trembling hands. Another turned to her partner and asked, "Please, would you mind..." before darting out of the room. The nurse who had delivered chest compressions looked terrorized as she washed traces of Eric's blood from her torn glove.

People barely spoke as they walked away from the scene. The chief nurse put her arms around a staff nurse and whispered something to her. Mrs. Green just sat in the chair near the desk muttering over and over, "Jesus. How dare you do this to me. Jesus..."

And there was Eric. Again. Resurrected back into hell. Teetering precariously on the outermost edge of life. The vision of his body as distorted spoiled fruit, skin covered with infections and dark split places, seared into the canvas behind my eyes. Yet, still, I found myself staring at him.

Moments later, I wasn't certain, but I thought I saw his lips move a little. I became transfixed, obsessively waiting for his smile to reappear. It was extremely subtle at first. But, then, in miniscule increments, the corners of his mouth began to rise above his chin once again while his mother continued to chant curses in the background. I had to leave.

I exited the ward and walked through the courtyard garden to the hospital administration building. I phoned two colleagues who were familiar with Eric's case. They told me that Eric's mother was to be obeyed; that she possessed the legal right to decide matters relating to his care; that Eric had agreed to her proxy; that the county did not want a lawsuit on its hands; that, yes, it was appalling and perverse.

I went to the bathroom to scrub my hands and throw cold water on my face. I did not know what to do. I felt trapped and dirty and traumatized. In the center of a maelstrom. I desperately needed to find sense within the horror. I needed to understand something about Eric and his mother—and me.

I called Lettie, the social worker. She told me that Mrs. Green had had a longstanding, hostile relationship with Eric, and that they had not seen each other in eleven years. Eric had been living on the streets, surviving as a male prostitute, and injecting heroin. When he was admitted to our hospital, he requested a hot meal, a toothbrush, a bag of corn chips, and a phone to call his mother. Mrs. Green arrived promptly the next morning in a colorful, elegant dress and a torrent of perfume. She entered Eric's room and immediately began to order the staff around. She unpacked a large bag full of her personal items and arranged them across her son's bedside stand. She donned a latex glove and touched her son's shoulder, saying only, "Eric, your mother is here." The social worker said that

that was the only time any staff had seen Mrs. Green touch Eric during the entire three weeks of her visit. Before he was first intubated, Eric told the social worker that he was happy his mother had come to visit him, and that he granted her full authority to make medical decisions for him. The discussion was dutifully witnessed by two nurses.

"Thanks, Lettie," I replied, disheartened.

"Doctor Scannell," she continued, "I think the staff is really suffering with this one. Mass post-traumatic stress disorder is around the corner."

"Yes, thanks again," I replied. "Listen, is there anyone who can talk to his mother?"

"No survivors, I'm sorry to report."

"Well, what about Eric?" I asked. "I have no idea who he is. Does anyone know him personally?"

"Doctor Scannell, no one besides his mother has come to visit. Eric told us that he had no friends. The outpatient clinic saw him only twice before he was hospitalized. Sorry again," she replied.

I returned to the hospital, visited other patients, and wrote medication orders that I double-checked against my distraction. I informed the head nurse that I had to postpone the staff meeting until a less hectic day, not revealing that all I was capable of managing at the time was moving, moment to moment, through my duties, as though clinging successively to one crosspiece and then the next on monkey bars.

That evening at home, I could not sleep most of the night. I imagined my eyes propped open by one crescented end of Eric's disturbing smile. At some point I drifted into sleep and dreamt of an enormous field strewn with the half-dead, bloodied bodies of many humans interspersed with those of a few sheep. The field was intersected by a red brick wall that had largely crumbled and scattered over the field. Just as a dream voice began explaining something to me about the nature of the collapsed wall and the "new sky forming overhead," my alarm clock sounded.

I arrived at work on automatic that morning, the habit of the drive delivering me to the hospital. At seven A.M. I found myself once again facing Mrs. Green and her grinning son. "Well," she greeted me, "you've finally come around to see us!"

She was sitting in a chair behind Eric's field of vision. Expensive dress suit. Thick layers of makeup that made her skin look like vinyl. I noticed that another chest tube had been placed through Eric's right rib cage. Apparently, his second lung had collapsed, and the ghastly medical ritual had continued to evolve. Little by little, organ by organ, pieces of Eric were crumbling.

I sat on his bed and held his cool, puffy hand. In front of his disparaging mother, I asked Eric one question after another. He indicated that he was not experiencing pain, that he had desired the second chest tube, and that he was pleased with his medical care. I quizzed him to ascertain if he was oriented to time and place. He nodded correctly to identify me and his nurse through a multiple-choice list of names. He knew he was dying from an incurable disease, and he was aware that his immune system and heart and lungs and kidneys were failing.

I was weary, physically and emotionally. I could hear his mother muttering in the background while I sat quietly next to Eric. I found myself hoping to gain some under-standing of the horror by sitting openly in its midst, receiving it rather than reacting to it, and just waiting with the questions. Why, I wondered, would any mother put her child through these harrowing procedures? Why would any son acquiesce to them? And how could I remove myself, as I must, from this nightmare?

But no clues offered themselves, no bridges to understanding were revealed. I turned to Mrs. Green and asked, "So, have you been here all night?"

"Yes," she replied, "*someone* has to watch over him in this place."

When I didn't react to her sarcasm, I realized that somehow I had acquired a modicum of distance from her. I prayed that it reflected the fruits of burgeoning personal insight and strength rather than the simple physical dulling from my fatigue.

"Yes, well, I suppose so," I responded perfunctorily and walked to the nurse's desk for Eric's chart. I scrawled several orders, resisting my impulse to strike large black X's across the pages.

As I wrote, Mrs. Green continued to complain about her son's care. She was particularly vexed about perceived delays in the rendering of various medical and nursing treatments to him. I told her that I had registered her complaints in the chart, and I volunteered the phone number she should call to complain formally to the state MediCal agency. I exited the room after bidding good-bye to Eric and his mother, feeling guilty about leaving the attendant nurse behind.

The remainder of the morning passed in a dense haze. During lunch, alone in the hospital courtyard, I remembered my strange dream. It had been so vivid. I concentrated, trying hard to recall the identities of the wounded bodies strewn across the field; to understand why there might be sheep present. After some confused reflection, I suspected the bloodied bodies might belong to Eric, me, Mrs. Green, and the staff.

I then remembered that some of the sheep had exhibited human faces. Oh, god, I thought, yes, each of us exists as both forms in the dream. Each of us lay wounded in our individual human circumstances, as banished son, guilty mother, scapegoated staff; and, simultaneously, we were together a sacrificial offering to a barbaric medical ritual serving Mrs. Green's gruesome ideals, her personal conflict.

I tried to dwell further on my dream, to focus on the field and look for more clues, since the field was where the great wall crumbled. I searched specifically for Mrs. Green in relation to her son. But my dream only evaporated the more I tried to identify individual bodies.

A throbbing headache began to ebb and flow across my skull. I finished lunch and returned automatically to Eric's room, although I didn't know what I might do or say once there.

When I arrived, Mrs. Green was reading the newspaper and sipping black coffee. She was surprised, I think, to see me there voluntarily, not as a result of my usual rounds or her summoning. She instantly started to complain about her son's bedsores and the intrusive beeping of the monitoring devices.

I took a deep breath and interrupted her. "Excuse me," I said calmly, "I need to speak with Eric." Ignoring her wide-eyed, arched-brow response, I sat next to him again and held one of his water-balloon hands.

"Eric, you really like having your mother here, don't you?" I asked.

He nodded.

"It probably feels really great to have her take care of you, doesn't it?"

"Yes," he indicated.

Mrs. Green suddenly became quiet. For the very first time, the three of us sat together in a silence. And this silence pulsed, almost painfully, like one shared frail heart among us.

I studied the strands of metal and plastic that pierced multiple sites on Eric's body. His tissues had become so fragile that it was nearly impossible to anchor intravenous lines to him anymore. Tape had sucked off patches of his skin, and the rubbing of soft hand restraints had created circular wounds around his wrists that looked like hand-cuff marks.

It felt as though time were suspended above us. I waited for it to move us all into the next moment. And, ultimately, it did. I ached while we waited, realizing what an awful price Eric was willing to pay to have his mother here with him. And, finally, to hear her voice insisting on his life.

"Eric," I said, "I think your mother is here because she desperately wants to be with you. She wants you to be alive for her. And she needs you to know this before you die."

At this, Eric's smile relaxed. Tears started to trail from the slit corners of his eyes. Mrs. Green turned her face away from us.

"Eric, I think your mother wishes for you to under-stand that she never completely gave you up. And now, at this very late time in your life, she just can't figure out how to let go of you."

Mrs. Green whimpered. The nurse blew her nose. I cried.

After holding Eric's hand a few more seconds, I walked to his chart and wrote new orders, for palliative measures only. I prescribed larger doses of morphine for his obvious pain. As I set my pen down, I noticed, with revulsion, that a piece of Eric's flesh was stuck like a potato peel on my palm. I hurried to the sink and tried to wash it away for a long while, but it felt as though it had grafted permanently onto my skin. When I eventually left the room, Mrs. Green rose from her station and followed me into the hallway.

"Doctor Scannell," she said.

I turned to meet her. I was completely calm facing her this time, and my authority surrounded me like a life preserver.

"Listen," she said, almost contrite, "I just want to make sure that he's getting decent care."

"Mrs. Green," I replied, "so do I."

She hung her head, and, shaking it back and forth, just kept making clicking sounds with her tongue against her teeth.

I said, "It's understandable that you want Eric to know he's still your child. That, despite everything that has happened between you two, you're still his mother."

She nodded.

I continued, "And it looks like Eric has wanted to have those experiences, too. But he's had them now. You've given them to him."

She still said nothing.

"Eric *knows*. You both know. Please, let him go now."

Several uneasy moments passed. "Mrs. Green," I said, "I need to inform you that I can't facilitate any more futile care for your son. I'd like to believe that, had I been here last night, I would have refused to torture Eric with that second chest tube. You can call all the newspapers, transfer your son to another hospital, or lodge any lawsuit you want."

Mrs. Green's clicking noises ceased. Then, without lifting her head, suddenly, she walked away.

I had no idea how our scene would ultimately play out. But at last I felt clarity and inner calm. Walking the hallway, I prayed for last-minute peace in Eric's life.

That evening at home, I continued to hope that before Eric died he and his mother would be able to recognize each other on their bloody field, identify the war between them and the common wound that separated them. I prayed that they could forgive themselves and each other.

All I know is what the night-shift nurses told me the next morning. They said that Eric's heart had flat lined again during the night, and that his mother had insisted that the on-call physician, unfamiliar with Eric's case, perform CPR. After twenty-four minutes of futile efforts, the physician pronounced that Eric was, at last, dead.

Mrs. Green just packed her bag, and, without bidding farewell to any staff, left the ICU immediately. No one ever heard from her again.

Years later, as I write this, I can still feel the place on my palm where Eric's skin stuck to mine. His smile continues to haunt me.

I also wonder about the staff who reluctantly bore witness to Eric's last days. I believe it is impossible that any of them has completely suppressed the nightmare. I have seen few things more terrible than what happened in that room: the brutal torture of someone under the guise of love.

At the very least, I want to believe that Eric was somehow finally comforted by his mother's presence. That, through her return to his life, Eric experienced himself reborn, if for only an instant, into the uncertain arms and gloved hands of a mother who had abandoned him.

I also want to believe that there are ways we can always locate one another on the same side of a wall, identify the wars between us and the truth of one another's suffering. I don't know, but I suspect that the field that holds these possibilities is the realm wherein we can sense one another's isolation and painful longing to be lovingly connected to the world and to other people.

But I am left, in the end, envisioning the way that Eric actually died: completely isolated, within the center of a bustling circle of physicians and nurses and technology, his mother yelling in the background. I picture how his body, finally dead, looked in the end, impaled and lifeless in that tangle of wires and lines. I am left imagining the sounds of Mrs. Green's high-heeled shoes striking the linoleum floor of the hospital corridor, echoing off its walls that night as she left the hospital alone.

Target Practice

Desire itself is movement.
—T. S. Eliot, Burnt Norton

"No, no. That's where I want to go," Marvin drawled.

"Are you sure, Marvin? I mean, we could take you to Macy's or Nordstrom's just as easily," Maggie offered.

"Or the beach, the ocean, the redwoods," I proposed.

Marvin seemed to be waiting patiently for us to stop talking. He was noisily chewing a piece of gum with rhythmic figure-of-eight movements of his jaw. "No. I just want to go to Target," he insisted.

"Is there something special you want to buy?" I asked.

"Just things," Marvin replied.

"Well, I could pick them up for you if you'd like," Maggie suggested. "Then maybe you could choose somewhere else for your big trip."

Marvin sighed deeply. "I like going to Target," he said.

Maggie and I looked at each other, raised our eyebrows, and shrugged our shoulders. We were finally reassured that Target was, indeed, the one place Marvin wished to visit before he died.

"Okay, Marvin," I said, "we'll start the wheels rolling. We'll try getting you to the blue-light special by the end of the week."

"There is no blue light at Target," he corrected me in a voice devoid of inflection. "That's K-Mart."

Maggie and I had been trying to do something nice for Marvin for days. Something that might give him pleasure. Shake him into liveliness, give him an animated presence.

It wasn't that we felt uncomfortable with his impending death. Rather, we were troubled by the kind of flatness in which he was living. His naturally rangy moods had collapsed into one thin band of neutrality. His sing-song voice had become monotone. The rhythm of his incessant gum chewing became maddeningly metronomic.

Even his physique tended toward the two-dimensional—his body dwindling away, shrinking, becoming one with his skeleton. Large brown trays stacked with industrially prepared foods in white microwave containers slipped untouched on and off his bedside table. The plastic hospital bracelet identifying Marvin by name and room number got larger and larger on his twiggy wrist.

The most poignant aspect of Marvin's attrition was his own apathy about it. When nurses routinely noted his untouched food trays, he'd respond, "Is that so?" without the inflection of an interrogative. Once on morning rounds I found him slumped in bed watching *I Love Lucy* while his intravenous line, accidentally disconnected from its catheter, dripped vitamin-fortified saline down his forearms and onto his soggy bed. I clamped the IV and exclaimed, "Marvin, you're getting all wet!" He replied dispassionately, "Oh, yes, so I am," continuing to stare straight ahead at Lucy.

Dementia and severe malnutrition had largely robbed Marvin of the capacity and energy to experience his own existence. He behaved like a disinterested audience watching his life happen as a dreadfully boring play on a remote stage.

Several staff members had tried to enliven Marvin in the past. They brought him interesting foods from foreign markets, offered to stroll with him through the hospital gardens, donated books of various genres, gave him massages, and arranged counseling opportunities. But an annihilative dullness continued to insulate Marvin from the life around and, seemingly, within him.

I suppose we could have reconciled ourselves to the void of Marvin's life; accepted it as a quiet, peaceful place from which he could coast easily into death, benumbed and undisturbed. Perhaps we were projecting our own needs too heavily on him, insisting that he sense his place in the world, feel us attached to him. Indeed, we probably needed something from Marvin, some confirmation reflecting the wondrous, precious felt experience of life. If he would not rage, at least we longed for him to blink against the dying of the light.

So you'd think that we would have welcomed without reservation Marvin's first pronouncement of *any* desire, even if it was a trip to Target. Mundane, pedestrian, uncelestial, fluorescent-lit Target that didn't even have blue-light specials. I think we were afraid to concede that the world could be so small; that one's last reach into life could be satisfied by an item on Target's shelves.

Dutifully, we contacted a local AIDS agency, which assigned a young volunteer to help us fulfill Marvin's request. The four of us decided on a day trip to the local Target the following Monday.

On Marvin's big day, I arrived early to round with him. I brought him the Sunday supplement, which contained a stunning array of Target specials. They even featured a sale on Wrigley chewing gum. "Here," I said, offering him the paper. "I hope you can use this."

"Thanks," he replied. With arms extended in front of him, he held the paper as though it were a wet puppy, at a distance, his shoulders to his ears, his arms jerky, his face troubled.

"They have a gum special," I recommended.

"No. I don't need any gum," he said.

"Oh," I replied, trying not to sound disappointed. "Well, what are you going to buy?"

"Things, is all."

"I think there's a special on those, too!" I declared, hoping for a smile.

But Marvin remained unflappable and replied, "Well, that's all right then," still trying to figure out how to relate to the newspaper.

Wanting to be helpful, I pointed to a couple of "things" that I thought might interest him. "Hey, there's a bargain on 'all ten-pack candy bars, ninety-seven cents,' and 'six-pack trouser socks, three-seventy-seven.' And, look, 'Four-ninety-seven for cotton canvas oxfords, lowest price of the season'."

Marvin laid the newspaper on his lap, and he suddenly appeared to recall certain behaviors that were associated with reading. He furrowed his brow and started to scan the paper. But, moments later, he was turning it upside down and sideways, scrutinizing it, as though he were examining a strange and dubious gem. "Hmm," he droned.

Most of the sale items I saw seemed superfluous to a dying man. The expensive GE phones, the VCRs, the

Advanced Photo System cameras—rather impractical investments. Pages of "children's wear at the lowest price of the season" symbolized bygone opportunities. A "decorative wall clock" would serve little active duty in Marvin's life. The "Scotchgard leather casuals," "electric-powered auto cleaners," "four-piece carpeted floor mat sets," and "nine-gallon portable air tanks" seemed like strange artifacts from a synthetic culture. And the "ab toner" was useless to ab-less Marvin.

After wishing him luck on his journey, I left Marvin's room to see other patients. Hours later, I ran into Maggie in the hallway. "How did Marvin's pilgrimage go?" I asked.

Maggie rolled her bulging, dewy eyes in a wide orbit. She made her pupils disappear behind her lids so that only the white parts showed. Her eyes reminded me of lychee nuts.

"He never made it," she reported, clicking her tongue for emphasis.

"What happened?" I asked.

"Well, our little volunteer had an asthma attack as she wheeled Marvin through the front door."

"She has a Target allergy? How unusual," I replied.

"No. She said they had a special on scented candles at the entrance. She's all right now. She's quieting down in the emergency room."

I returned to Marvin's room, pushing aside the blue canvas curtain that hung by dull chrome hooks from a metal bar, ostensibly separating Marvin from his roommate. These curtain dividers symbolized privacy, and we drew them closed when we wished to pretend that we were secluded. Yet anyone behind the canvas could easily hear your every hushed word, the intimacies of your bowel and bladder, your cries and moans, your visitors, your telephone conversations, the dietician's recitations of your dinner menu, the rumblings of mucus in your throat, your doctor's discussions of your internal organs. Your life was made completely naked by that curtain.

Inside our blue shroud, Marvin was propped upright in bed, still clutching his shopping list and a small zippered pocketbook. "Marvin, I'm so sorry. I heard what happened this morning."

"Yeah, well, that's all right," he reported laconically.

"Want to try again tomorrow?" I asked.

"Yeah," he replied.

I was excited that Marvin still had enough desire to venture forth again. I glanced at his list, curious, wanting to ascertain the items on it. But he had folded in a way that obscured his writing.

Maggie entered the room and announced, "All right. We have a different volunteer coming tomorrow at eleven o'clock. Is that okay, Marvin?"

Marvin nodded.

As we left the room together, I asked Maggie if she knew what was written on Marvin's shopping list. "Who knows? Things," she said.

That next day, due to medical urgencies on the ward, I was not able to see Marvin before he left. Hours after his scheduled excursion, about three in the afternoon, I emerged from a family conference in the intensive-care room and spotted Maggie at the end of the hallway, pulling the hair on her scalp with clenched fists, bugging her eyes.

I approached her, and, to make a small contribution to her apparent insanity, I nonchalantly passed her by.

"No!" she proclaimed. "You're not getting away that easily. This was *your* idea."

"What?" I asked innocently.

"Listen. Marvin and the volunteer got as far as our parking lot..."

I interrupted, "and the volunteer got leprosy?"

"No, the volunteer couldn't get Marvin's wheelchair into his little sports car. It was too big for the door."

I had seen Marvin wobbling in that wheelchair before. He embodied my own personal best attempt at drawing the human form—a stick figure. He sat in the chair, barely bowing its leather sling, appearing lost in space. "Can we get him a pediatric chair?" I asked.

"Yes," Maggie replied, "we'll have to request one special. And all the paperwork authorizing Marvin's pass has to be redone."

"Oh, good," I replied, "it'll give us something to do besides attending to dreadful diseases."

Two days later, one healthy volunteer, a small wheelchair, and official permits were ready for Marvin's junket to Target. The weekly specials were still valid.

"Marvin, short of an earthquake, I think this trip to Target is going to work," I said. "Do you still want to go?"

"Yes, yes, I do," he replied in monotone.

With my fingers I combed back the few thready strands of his brown hair that hung from his temples like limp, sad tassels. "Are you ready?" I asked.

He nodded.

"Got your list?" I asked.

Marvin extended his hand toward me, demonstrating the crumpled notepaper wadded up within his damp fist. I had become intensely curious about his list, and I decided to return at the end of the day, hoping he'd be interested in a shared viewing of his new treasures.

I walked to the nursing station and found Maggie. She said, "If this doesn't happen today, it's not going to happen at all. Three times. That's it."

"I wouldn't be so rigid if I were you," I replied.

"Listen, *doctor*," Maggie scowled, "we don't have time to take patients *shopping*. In case you haven't noticed, there is a lot of work to be done around here. Nursing work. Like medications and IVs and…"

"Maggie," I interrupted, "I'm saying this only for your own good. Be careful. I wouldn't stand in the way."

"What do you mean?" she asked.

"Well, did you get a look at the advertisements in the Sunday supplement?"

"I didn't actually read them. Why?" she asked.

"All I'm saying, Maggie, is that there were an awful lot of sevens and nines in the prices."

"So what?"

"Well, this Target thing could be a cult," I responded. "It might be dangerous for you to interfere."

Maggie ceased her frantic sorting of lab slips and stared at me until I realized I should leave.

Hours later, en route to the radiology department, I spotted Maggie, arms akimbo, eyes pure white, standing at the nursing station behind Marvin's wheelchair. I watched as Marvin's sandpiper legs moved him cyclically frontward and then backward in the chair, in sum, causing him to remain in the same place. The metal foot rests had been removed so that Marvin's slippered feet rested on the floor.

"Slouching toward Target?" I whispered to Maggie.

She suddenly appeared homicidal. Through gritted teeth she staccatoed, "There are no footrests on this g.d. chair."

"How long have the two of you been here?" I asked.

Luckily, just then, as Maggie's face turned crimson until she looked like an agitated tomato, and while Marvin earnestly continued to pedal himself toward the same spot, the volunteer appeared in the hallway.

"Thank goodness you're here," I welcomed him. "The moment was ripe for disaster."

Maggie left. The volunteer and I placed an extra pair of slippers over Marvin's feet and turned the wheelchair backward, pulling Marvin smoothly along the hallway, his heels protected.

Throughout the rest of the day I was distracted often by thoughts of Marvin's pilgrimage. It had been wonderful to see a faint glimmer of desire, a hint of the seeker in him. I began imagining what I might designate as my own "last request." I guessed that Maggie's might have been to get Marvin through Target's doors. Mine, I decided, would be a trip to Ireland with an intimate friend who was also a professional masseuse. Who could make me laugh. Who thrived on planning all the travel arrangements. Who would drive the car.

At the end of the work day, I returned to Marvin's room.

"Marvin?" I announced myself.

But there was no reply. I parted the blue curtain and found him motionless in bed, eyes rolled upward, mouth hung wide open. "No!" I gasped, horrified at the possibility that Marvin might have been stalling death for Target. Frantically, I rattled his bony shoulder.

To my immediate relief, he awoke. "Oh, Marvin," I managed to say as my heart rate began to slow toward physiologic range.

"Uh, hi," he muttered.

He stared at me impassively, two of his perhaps dozen hairs fallen into his eyes. I pushed them aside.

"So how was your trip to Target?" I asked.

Marvin cleared his throat. I could hear someone drumming his fingers against the nightstand in the other half of the semiprivate room.

"It was nice. Very nice," he replied with the dramatic inflections of someone reading microwave instructions.

I scouted the room for Marvin's new "things" or a Target shopping bag. But I saw neither. Now I was fiercely curious about the mysterious items on his list, craving their identity as clues that would help me understand Marvin's last request and the nature of his final attachments to the external world.

"What did you get?" I asked.

"Nothing," he replied.

"Did you make it inside the store this time? Safely?"

"Yeah."

"And, really, you bought nothing?" I asked.

"I bought nothing," he responded.

"What about the things on your list?"

"Yeah."

"I mean," I explained, "weren't they things that you needed?"

He shrugged.

"Would you like to try again? Maybe Sears this time? Or K-Mart?" I suggested.

"No. I'm fine," he replied.

"Marvin, I have to stop at the stores on the way home tonight. Maybe I could find the things you need."

He looked at the list clumped within his palm and said, "No. No, thank you."

I tried to resign myself to the fact that Marvin was satisfied. With Target. With his lack of purchases. I also relinquished hope that I would ever know what Marvin listed as those vestiges of the world he'd wished to own. Those few earthly remnants that called forth his final desire.

About one week later, on morning rounds, I found Marvin dead, sprawled over his green hospital blanket. He appeared to have died a couple of hours earlier. I pushed the strings of his hair back across his scalp, closed his eyelids, and sat in the chair near his bed, watching him for a few minutes. The room was still dark, waiting for sunrise. The patient in the next bed was snoring. The morning shift of nurses was assembling in the break room outside.

At that moment, I felt deeply grateful for Marvin's gentle presence on our ward. For the ways he managed to spark my own desire—for my work and avocation. For the the ways he allowed me into his life. "Good-bye, Marvin. Thank you," I said quietly, aloud.

I kissed his forehead and, rising to leave, I noticed a crumpled wad of notepaper on his bedside table, half hidden by a twelve pack of gum. I recognized it as Marvin's shopping list.

I hesitated a while. I debated the pros and cons of sneaking a peek. I searched Marvin's impassive face for guidance. And finally I decided to look.

Sitting down on Marvin's bed, I touched his hand and examined his face once more for any sign of instruction. I then carefully unraveled his tattered list as though I were unfurling an ancient, fragile treasure map. And there, in the center of the rumpled page, in smudged pencil scrawling, was written "htings."

A Form of Motherhood
Journal entry, 1987

The clouds change perpetually over our houses. I do this,
do that, and again do this and then that. Meeting and parting,
we assemble different forms, make different patterns.
—Virginia Woolf, The Waves

I created a perfect snow angel once. 1958. Michigan. I
threw my five-year-old body into a new bed of snow that
seemed to be waiting for me behind our garage. It was that
crisp kind of snow that crackled when you stepped into it.
That remembered your footprint or mittened hand precisely. I leaped from the neighbors' cyclone fence and
sailed through the frigid air in my plum-colored penguin-
shaped snow suit, arms spread out like stubby wings. I
landed flat, facedown in the snow bank. The crunch I
heard was a wonderful singular sound confirming a perfect, all-points-simultaneous landing. I moved my arms up
and down once and brought my red rubber boots together.
Trying not to disturb my snow angel, I slowly, carefully,
rose from its flawless interior and jumped outside of it.
Standing several inches away, my cheeks frozen, my
breath creating white curls of frost, I admired its perfect
form. The sun sparkled through the splinters of ice crys-

tals dangling on the razor-sharp outline of my angel. I was amazed that life could be so magnificent.

Three decades later, it is December in California. The seasons are understated here. Residents still reminisce about the day it snowed in San Francisco many years ago. It has been raining continuously for days. I am standing before Kenny's empty bed. Already it has been prepared for another patient. The percale sheets are impossibly white, cleansed completely of memory of the body that lay here just yesterday.

Yesterday. I stood in this same place, next to Kenny. Everything in the room and outside the window had seemed gray. Slate-colored pigeons pressed against the pane, oblivious to the rain collecting on the sill where they perched and to the slow process of death on this side of the window. They pushed their puffed bellies against the glass, making round, flat circles of dull feathers. They snapped their necks in multiple directions, always keeping one dark eye to the interior of this room. In certain moments the fluorescent light from the ceiling revealed their wings to be metallic green, the color of meat turning.

Kenny's room was filled with three sounds. The sucking, fluttering noises from his throat as he halfheartedly pulled air into his lungs. The motorized whir of the intravenous pump forcing water and salt into his veins. The high-pitched wobbling of vowels from the hollow throats of the pigeons outside. On rare occasions, Kenny roused, and there was the rustling of heavily starched sheets and the crackling of his blue plastic mattress.

Mrs. Cahill, Kenny's mother, had visited him one week ago. She stood exactly where I now stand. She had traveled from Iowa, alone, after I phoned her one week earlier to inform her that her son was ill, dying from lymphoma, a cancer of the lymph glands that occurs in some people with AIDS. The last time she had seen her son was eight years ago, when he was seventeen years old. It was then that she and her new husband, Kenny's stepfather, banished Kenny from their home. They would not tolerate his presence in their lives, their house, if he "continued to be gay."

Mrs. Cahill remarked on the phone that she had been unaware that her son had AIDS. At first, she remained silent when I mentioned that Kenny's only request was to see her one final time. After a long pause, she agreed to visit.

When Mrs. Cahill arrived seven days later, she was identifiable instantly as Kenny's mother, sharing with him alabaster skin, rust-colored hair, and sea-green eyes. When we met, she stood stiffly, greeting me with, "The way you spoke on the phone last week, I had assumed he'd be dead by now."

She seemed irritated, disappointed that Kenny was still alive. Her voice sounded stifled and mid-throated, as though her anger had been muffled by a mighty hand. Deep facial lines formed sad concentric circles around the downturned corners of her mouth, looking like waves fanning outward from a center where something had been dropped, submerged. She kept the muscles around her neck and shoulders contracted, and her posture in almost-perfect vertical alignment. Her extreme thinness made her appear two-dimensional, like one of those flat, vinyl Color-form figures; her rigidity was accentuated against the background scene of the ward, of her son's predicament, where everything moved in fluid dimensions of life and death. Standing a few feet from Kenny's bed, her figure cut a sharp-edged outline; when I ushered her out of his room, into the hallway, it seemed as though her shadowy imprint stayed behind.

In the ward hallway I explained that it was impossible to predict precisely when someone would die. All I could tell her was that her son's death was imminent. And that he just wanted to see her once more.

"Fine time to be wanting that," she snapped.

I was stunned. I had seen parents, drawn urgently to their dying children's bedsides, exhibit all sorts of chaotic emotion; but I had yet to witness such bitterness from a mother—at least from one who actually responded to her son's request for a visitation. Hoping that she was temporarily confused with grief, momentarily bewildered by the uncertainties of her son's condition or the estrangement between them, I said, "Mrs. Cahill, Kenny told me that he *has* wanted to see you for a very long time."

She clicked her tongue against her teeth and staccatoed, "Well, all he had to do was to stop being gay. It was that simple. We would've taken him right back into our home and into our family. It doesn't seem like much to ask of someone in return for an entire family." She stared directly into my eyes with a certainty and sharpness that neatly parted the world into black and white.

Her clarity awed me. I thought how much easier it would be to live life if all experience and understanding could be so neat and monochrome. "Mrs. Cahill," I said, "you know, it's not that simple. People don't just choose their sexuality."

She looked away from me, fixing one frosty eye to my face, and she muttered, "Of course they do. And *most* of us live by the rules."

None of the men and women I knew who were gay-identified ever felt as though they had chosen their sexuality. In fact, many of them suffered from their inability to deny it, and they struggled against it because they feared sociopolitical repercussions, loss of family unity, and job discrimination. I had never heard of people choosing to be heterosexual. Each of us seemed to have a truth in our bodies and hearts that could not be chosen or bent without inflicting terrible damage on our lives. But this was neither the place nor time to discuss such topics with Mrs. Cahill.

"Your son just wants to see you before he dies. You don't have to settle that issue with him now."

She replied, "If there are forms that need to be filled out, I should do them now. I'll be leaving for Iowa in a few hours."

"There are no forms," I replied.

"Well, fine then," she said. "I don't have much time anyway."

"No, there's not much time, is there? What are you going to do with the time you have left?" I asked.

She rolled her eyes. "Listen," she said, "my husband— Kenny's stepfather—would throw a fit if he knew that I was here visiting Kenny. He thinks I'm with my sister in Seattle. He's a good man. A law-abiding, religious man who believes that I shouldn't consider Kenny my son as long as Kenny decides to stay the way he is. And my husband has an excellent point, because it's true that *I* never raised a gay son. *I* raised a *normal* son. Not that boy in that room who has that AIDS thing. And in my heart, I know that AIDS is a punishment, surely, for...for being gay."

"Mrs. Cahill," I replied, stunned again, "you can't believe that. People don't get sick or stay healthy because they're good or bad. Even you and your 'good husband' will get ill and die eventually."

Instantly, Mrs. Cahill turned angry. She bitterly reproached me with, "Well, *you* don't have a son or daughter, do you, Doctor Scannell?"

"No," I responded, feeling defensive, aware that she was about to attack the authenticity of any opinion I might have on the matters of mothers and children. "I don't have children."

"So," she said, matter-of-factly, "you can't possibly understand what I'm talking about. You couldn't know what it's like to give birth to a child who sheds the skin you gave him—nature gave him, *God* gave him—who walks up to you one day, acting like nothing in the world has happened, and announces, 'Hey, I'm gay now.' And there he stands in your doorway, in a completely different, unnatural skin, and assumes that you should recognize him just like before, still your son. Doctor Scannell, you can't *possibly* understand."

Our discussion was stuck at an impasse. "Don't talk to me until after you've had children of your own," she muttered.

I replied, "It's true that I won't ever have the experience of being a mother. But I still know what it's like to be badly disappointed by people you love. And I also know that it's possible to forgive them."

"Well," she replied, her fingers hooked to mimic quotation marks, "this 'disappointment' can be righted immediately, if he simply chooses to give up being gay. That's the only thing that's necessary. He has a choice, and he knows it. And even now, he has chosen not to be saved."

"You asked him just now?" was all I could manage.

"Of course," she replied.

"Is that the only thing you discussed?" I asked.

"There's no bad time to be saved," she said.

It was always agonizing to watch people sacrifice their hearts to comply with rules and religion and principle. In my medical practice, at the deathbeds, I had never known anyone opting for principle over love who did not ultimately suffer terrible and, usually, irreconcilable regret. Around Kenny and his mother, I felt as though I were audience to the reunion of two people at the site of an old, private tragedy: the burial place of their two wrecked lives. They seemed drawn together now if only to bear witness to their immutable suffering and irredeemable pain.

"Mrs. Cahill," I pleaded, "isn't there some other way of being with Kenny now? As a mother? This can't be how you want to remember the last time with him," I said.

But she turned away from me, declaring, "Well, yes, it is. What you don't seem to accept, doctor, is that Kenny has been dead to me for many years already." And she walked away.

Yesterday, one week after her visit, I sat near Kenny's bed and watched him breathe as if he had forgotten how. He sucked in air haltingly and irregularly.

Between us seemed to hover the flat, shadowy outline his mother left in the room. Like a dark, sinister angel over his body, claiming him. As I imagined looking into it, I remembered her comment to me about not having children of my own and, therefore, not being able to understand some profound aspect of life and love. Her words stung and made me feel insecure, and I wondered if she could be right, if my life was intrinsically flawed and diminished without children.

Meanwhile, Kenny's life was fading, and he lay alone and motherless in his bed. I rose from my chair and walked to the bedside where Mrs. Cahill's specter still stood; I stepped inside her outline and paused there a few seconds. Then I began to fill it with my own body; I took in deep breaths, stood straight and tall, stretched against the outline, bent its contours. I imagined my arms thickening like soft rolls of pastry dough rising, my waist expanding into a supple mound, and my breasts enlarging across my chest. I felt like me—just more so. Then I sat on Kenny's bed and watched over him a while. He looked so small in his oversized hospital gown and awkwardly fitted diaper.

"Kenny," I whispered, "open your eyes if you can."

He did, though his eyes were heavy with foggy sleep. I scooped him up into my massive arms, and I rocked him back and forth. With his head on my shoulder he cried until he fell asleep. Then I laid him down, and pulling the blanket under his chin, I left.

Cruising with Mother Teresa

*Everything happens to everybody sooner or
later if there is time enough.*
—George Bernard Shaw, Back to Methuselah

"No, Thomas, you can't cruise in front of Mother Teresa!
That's terrible. I don't like it at all. You know she's almost
a saint. Please promise you won't," pleaded Gregory. He
tugged the small crucifix on his gold neck chain as though
invoking authority.

Thomas' eyes widened and rolled like two pinwheels,
causing the thick crusts of herpes lesions on his forehead
to crack. With his neck extended, his lips pulled downward in a mock grimace, and his voice dropped into a
deeply resonant baritone, he replied indignantly, "Listen,
girl, there will be lots of cute sisters at that reception. If
you're silly enough to ignore them, then you deserve to
remain your sorry single self. *I'm* gonna get me a piece of
heaven."

Gregory shook his prematurely bald head and said,
"You know, you're such a stereotype, Thomas. You
embarrass me."

"Guys, can't you act civil with each other? You two
always sound like you're married or something," interjected

one-eyed Bill. A viral infection had blinded his right eye weeks earlier.

"Ha! Married! I've never been that desperate," Thomas replied.

Steven, generally silent during group meetings, cleared his throat and, almost apologetically, said, "Thomas, I think Gregory's right. It's disrespectful to her."

The men in the room stared at Steven as though they had just seen the holy virgin appear in a taco shell.

Thomas broke the silence. "Why, it's a miracle! He can speak!"

"No, man, it's true," Gregory insisted. "You know it's got to be one of those bad sins. One of the big ones. What are they called? 'Cardinal,' maybe? Or 'original'? I forget, but you don't have much space left in your soul for another sin, Thomas, really. Your milk bottle is almost completely black."

"What fool nonsense are you talking about? What milk bottle?"

"You know, how your soul is like a bottle of milk. The kind that comes in glass bottles. And every time you sin there's another black spot inside it."

"Not only are you foolish," admonished Thomas, "but you're a petty racist."

"What? Are you calling this Chicano a racist?" Gregory challenged, pointing a finger to himself. Then, turning to me, he asked, "Doctor Scannell, don't you think it's wrong to cruise in front of Mother Teresa?"

I had never considered this particular dilemma. Nonetheless, having been educated in Catholic schools, I was highly practiced in the contemplation of bizarre scenarios that begged an ethical or moral decision. Indeed, I was famous in grammar school for my ability to resolve the most complex and disturbing vignettes that the nuns could muster. I knew how to respond correctly should a man ever jump from behind a bush demanding that I either relinquish my Catholic faith or suffer death by fifteen stab wounds with an unclean butcher knife. In second grade I waxed eloquent about the crisis of faith posed should God himself appear before me and ask me to stop believing in him. I successfully negotiated one of the sisters' most notorious vignettes: what to do should one discover that one's best girlfriend chewed the host. And I was quite certain that I knew the right answer should I ever encounter a man asking me to lie to my parents in exchange for a lifetime of candy.

But the notion of looking for romance, let alone sexual affection, in front of a nun immediately constricted me. "I'm sorry, but I can't even imagine that," I replied. "And, frankly, I really, really don't want to."

One-eyed Bill interjected, "I just want to touch her hand. I heard she can perform miracles. Maybe she can make me see again."

Everyone fell silent and looked at Bill. Then a soft chorus of "yeah" and "amen" filled the room.

Kurt, deaf from complications of meningitis suffered in childhood, had remained quiet in the corner of the room during the entire conversation. I wondered how much of the strange discussion he understood. The stated purpose of our meeting had been that of planning a group visitation with Mother Teresa at the local Center for AIDS Services the following week.

"Kurt," I said through exaggerated lip choreography, "have you decided whether or not you're going?"

Simultaneously, Kurt's hands and mouth moved, replying, "Yes, but I want Jack to come with me." Jack was his partner of fifteen years upon whom, in the later debilitating stages of AIDS, Kurt became progressively dependent for interpretations of the aural world. Jack had this funny way of translating things that seemed suspiciously like shorthand to me. Once he conveyed my long-winded explanation of cryptococcal meningitis to Kurt with what seemed to be a few brief flickers of his fingers that could have passed for a nervous tic.

"That's fine," I replied. "There should be room in the van."

"You know," Gregory interjected, "Mother has those dreamy eyes like Robert DeNiro. Dark and very intense. I saw them on television once."

"Oh, and I adore the way she dresses," added Thomas. "I want to get me some of those long, flowing veils and maybe one of those necklaces with the beautiful glass beads."

"Those beads are a rosary, Thomas. A rosary! You know, I really think you should stop mocking everything. It makes me feel creepy, like I'm guilty of a sacrilege just being around when you talk like that."

"Ha! You *are* a sacrilege. How do you think you got here in the first place, you harlot?"

Gregory's face alternated between expressions of infuriation and defeat, settling upon something that looked like sadness.

"Okay, okay," I interrupted, "I'm going to referee you guys. It's time out with this nonsense. Let's talk about our trip now."

One-eyed Bill, sitting atop a floor pillow, rolled his unpatched eye upward and said uneasily, "I don't want to meet Mother Teresa if I'm wearing a diaper."

The room fell quiet again. Everyone looked to me, expectantly. I wanted to reassure Bill, but I wasn't certain that I could console a grown man about the possibility of soiling himself publicly, especially before a dignitary. Thomas looked at his feet, and Gregory started swinging his crucifix from a knuckle of chain. Kurt and Steven exchanged grimaces.

I thought how each of these men would be meeting Mother Teresa with a body branded by AIDS. Thomas with herpetic, crablike skin covering most of his face and torso. Gregory with his skeletal body and dark sunken eyes that disturbed people, presumably with the enormity of their hunger. Kurt with big purple splotches of Kaposi's sarcoma circling his eyes and mouth. Steven with multiple infections that have propelled him through time to his status as a weathered, gray-haired man in a wheel chair.

My vocal cords knotted, and I instructed myself not to cry. I took a deep, steadying breath and exhaled, "You guys look beautiful to me."

After another brief silence I said, "Bill, I think Mother Teresa has a big mole on her face. And bad teeth."

Bill looked at me delighted and shocked, as though I had uttered a bad word. Then, with his good eye, he spanned the faces of the men in the room, provoking their laughter.

"You know, you might be right, doc," Gregory exclaimed.

"Are you sure you're not thinking of Golda Meir?" asked Thomas seriously.

"Well, perhaps they both have moles. I'm not certain—Wait a minute, that's not the point," I said.

"Doc," Bill offered, "you're trying to say like we all have bad teeth and things on our face."

"Yes, that's what I'm trying to say," I replied.

Then, from what seemed to be my blind spot, came Gregory's question: "Doctor Scannell, where are your moles?"

There was that terrible moment again, when everyone looked at me and waited for my uncertain response. I thought about the other talent I had perfected during my Catholic education, the ability to criticize myself with unchristianlike abandon. I thought about my peculiar C-shaped legs that often bumped into each other like confused half moons; how my vanity hindered me from wearing shorts in even the most tropical climates. I could indicate my raccoon eyes and recount the teasing I endured from grammar-school boys. Perhaps exhibit my surgically distorted knee. Or reveal my pear-shaped body. Still, I knew these complaints were different; they were not tribal markings of a dying man or the letter on the forehead publicly exposing or insinuating private acts of one's genitals.

"Well, guys," I began, "I know it's different, but I have been ashamed of many parts of my body, even my entire body, at various times. My legs are terribly bowed, the dark circles under my eyes frighten small children, and I strongly suspect that one of my real parents was a Bartlett pear. But, of course, my worst moles are very deep. Internal."

At this point I believed that I had revealed myself adequately, intimately, and I hoped that we could move forward to the task of organizing our trip.

But then Gregory persisted with, "Like what?"

I was trying to decide whether or not I wanted to air my "sins" to these men. I had not gone to confession in many years. When I was seventeen, I decided that I'd never again make confession to a Catholic clergy; with the shrill passion of a teenage vignette queen suddenly politicized and disillusioned by organized religion, I told the nuns that I would not confess my sins until the Church confessed its own offenses. And that included its acknowledgment of its heartless attitude toward its gay community.

I was remembering this incident as I looked around the room at these men who desperately wanted to touch Mother Teresa's hand. I thought how amazing it was that they would still reach for her within the context of a religion that condemned the ways in which they've loved. And I thought how astounding, how truly beautiful was this nun, this woman whose arms, sleeved in the uniform of the Catholic Church, would reach beyond her religion into a larger faith in humanity that lovingly embraced these men.

"Gregory," I said, "you're really driving me insane. Let's just say that I could benefit from a few hours in a confessional. Or on a therapist's couch."

"Hmm," began Thomas, "why don't we all go to the exorcist together on our next field trip?"

"Okay," said Gregory, "but you have to go last, Thomas, so the rest of us can get seen."

Then they all started laughing and throwing pillows at one another. And watching them, I thought, of course—another vignette: What would you do if someone told you that Mother Teresa was coming to town and you had to organize an exotic group of men who...

Books on a Map

And you O my soul where you stand,
Surrounded, detached, in measureless oceans of space,
Ceaselessly musing, venturing, throwing,
seeking the spheres to connect them,
Till the bridge you will need be formed,
till the ductile anchor hold,
Till the gossamer thread you fling catch somewhere, O my soul.
—WALT WHITMAN, SONG OF MYSELF

"I *need* to get the books on a map," he insisted again.

"What books?" I asked. "What map, Mark?"

His jaw clenched, his eyes narrowed to coin slots, and his nostrils expanded into miniature bugles. He cupped his hands around his skull as though needing to contain it. "The books!" he cried. "I...I need to get them on the map! *Now*!"

For several weeks Mark had been wandering alone within a solitary and insulated world. He offered no evidence that he received signals from those of us on the outside. He remained mute but for the occasional strange bridge of words that he'd suddenly lay out before us— always a treacherous construction, beckoning us to travel to common ground but certain to leave us stranded, suspended somewhere along its span. His sentences were chaotic and unstable creations, their words lacking dependable linkages. Still, I thought, if I understood Mark's anxieties about his books and his maps, I might be able to help him. But the opportunities flickered unpredictably, and the bridges collapsed within seconds, leaving Mark sealed within his tiny, self-reflecting universe once again.

It was jarring to watch him flit in and out of awareness, his body enduring, intact, warm. He had remained ruggedly handsome throughout his years of coexisting with the AIDS virus. Fine lines, like delicate seashell striations, fanned from the corners of his tobacco-brown eyes. Even the virus respected his physical beauty, declining to leave traces on his exterior. It seemed a ruse, Mark popping out occasionally from his healthy-looking body like a disturbed jack-in-the-box bearing confused tidings.

Mark had been an accountant before the AIDS virus had left hazardous sinkholes across the landscape of his brain. Over months his memory slid into them, disappearing slowly and steadily. His personality followed within weeks. Finally, those primitive brain cells that spark awareness when simply rubbed against the outer world were sucked so completely into the sinkholes that they lost contact with the exterior realm. Clumped together in small pockets in the depths, they rubbed only against one another, creating internal circuits of self-stimulation. Diagnostic scans evaluating Mark's dementia revealed his brain to be atrophied; they could not locate his intellect or personality within the dark, sequestered places.

The erasure of personhood is a stunning thing to witness. You stand by helplessly, watching the normal invitations into that person's life—shared aesthetics, intellectual ventures, humor, romantic or soulful feelings, emotional interplay—simply evaporate. The powerlessness of a person's psyche against a submicroscopic virus chills. The frailty of human interrelatedness disturbs.

Mark's rare and fleeting ventures into speech always exuded impatience and agitation. His face twitched and frowned during his restless silences. His perpetual consternation agonized me. He seemed like a helpless child, roaming lost and afraid without language. I wondered if his frustration sounded from desire rubbing against his ability to speak, a glass barrier between them. Then again, perhaps Mark actually thought that he *was* expressing himself coherently and that we outsiders were inert, incapable recipients.

The "books" and the "maps." Was he speaking imagistically or metaphorically? Were those ways that perception and experience were encoded once neurologically unhooked from the obtuse conventions of literal mindedness?

The books, I imagined, might be his accounting logs. Those precisely ruled sheets of paper carrying the tension between what is due and what is owed, demanding symmetry and balance. If Mark retained a modicum of self-awareness, surely he was agitated by the frustrating imbalance in his neural accounting, the uncompensated, steady loss of his brain cells.

Yet, perhaps his books were books of stories. Favorite tales, comforting words, entertaining experiences. Accounts of other peoples' lives.

I could conceive no other meaning for "map" than that of a representation of territory. Mark's flickering agitation inferred that he was lost and distressed, wanting location. Of himself and his books.

Finally, after multiple unsuccessful attempts to understand Mark's desperate plea, I just said, "Yes. Okay. We'll get all your books on a map. All of them."

Mark quieted, but he regarded me suspiciously. Uncertainty kept his eyes in motion, traveling back and forth to my face, searching for evidence as to whether or not I could be trusted. And then, like the shadow image of the universe bursting into existence billions of years ago, Mark poofed away, vanished, into his interior.

Several days later, Mark's mother arrived. A time-worn, ancestral woman whose neck bent forward with the weight of her head. We met at Mark's bedside where she stood gazing at him, stroking his forehead as though he had just come home from kindergarten with the flu. I had seen so many women bent over their dying sons like this. Their posture, their form, seemed carved from an ancient stone that could crush a heart, that sounded a timeless melancholy witnessed through centuries.

"Hello. Mrs. Warner?" I asked.

Her head bobbed rhythmically up and down. She indicated yes by closing her eyes and smiling. After introducing ourselves, she asked me to step into the hallway with her, explaining, "I don't want him to hear us."

Outside Mark's door, she declined the offer of a chair from one of the nurses who passed us by, and, like me, wanted to lend her support. Steadying herself with one hand against the wall and the other on her pale wooden cane, she confided in a wobbly whisper, "You know, Doctor Scannell, Mark is gay. But he used to be married."

"Yes," I replied, "I know that. His personal history is recorded in the medical record."

She repositioned her hand on the wall to better steady herself and, after clearing her rusty throat, added, "And he has two teenage sons."

"Yes, your grandsons," I responded. "They look a lot like Mark. They visited him yesterday."

Appearing suddenly forlorn, she turned sideways to peer into her son's room as though checking in on him. She then fortified herself with a deep, noisy breath and said, "Doctor, my son was doing pretty well until three years ago. That's when they laid him off his job at the bank. They told him that they were just letting go of lots of people, that it had nothing to do with him having AIDS. Maybe that's true. I don't know. I don't really know."

I nodded in sympathy. I had known many people who found themselves instantly unemployed when their HIV infection was discovered by their employers.

"Well," she continued, "he lost all his self-respect after that. He became depressed. Very depressed. He sometimes just sat in my kitchen, at the table, mumbling for hours about his life being over. There being no point left to anything. He spent all his savings within months and had to move in with me. A year ago, he started getting sick. Very tired, and weak—like me. Imagine that."

I did. I thought of Mrs. Warner's soft bones and floppy muscles. Of how canes and walls and chairs had partially replaced them as structural support. Although Mark retained a strong skeleton and bulky musculature, they could not move him through the world, dependent as they were on assignment and direction dispatched from his mind, which had largely abandoned concern for his flesh.

"I'm so sorry," I replied. "Watching a son die must be…"

Suddenly, Mrs. Warner began to cry quietly. I was poised to put my arm around her, but she motioned for me to keep a distance. I felt embarrassed. I wondered if she considered me too young to comfort her. Unable to understand her particular agony. Perhaps my gesture was too familiar. Perhaps doctors didn't do that kind of thing in her old-world scheme.

She tried to speak, but she choked and swallowed most of her words. Finally, she calmed and managed, "Doctor, my son slept with a handgun under his pillow all last year." And with that her body began to quake in great, rueful sobs. She moaned and she cried, "I waited, the whole year, every night, to hear that gun go off. Oh, my god! My god! I lay in my bed awake so many nights…I kept imagining…I was so afraid to find him one day…"

Piercing my heart was the vision of two women standing together: one, a young mother listening for her infant boy's cries from a cradle in the next room and the other, an ancient woman listening for a gunshot from her man-boy's bedroom.

I felt my heart spiral downward, like a bird winged in flight and descending. It dropped to my stomach, leaving a cold, hollow space in my chest into which Mrs. Warner's cries entered. Her cries vibrated that space, agitating, dislodging, disturbing old wounds within that I thought were firmly scarred over. All the deaths and suffering I had witnessed on the AIDS ward and hoped to have contained were split wide open again. Bleeding from reopened wounds were the revived images of particular patients, their friends, their families. An old woman, sobbing, leaning on a thin stick of wood, and a young man with a handgun under his pillow were joining the raw interior places that I thought could not accommodate any more. And then it felt as though all the painful images, old and new, began to merge into one great awful ache, and pain stripped bare of words flooded me.

The old woman's bones seemed to loosen from the impact of her wailing. The wall and the cane were not supporting her. She started to bend further forward, and I thought she might be slumping toward the chair across the hall. But she turned to me instead and fell into my arms. I embraced her as though I alone were keeping her physically intact.

Within our embrace, I felt us to be formless and faceless, a vaporous undifferentiated pain. I could only repeat, over and over, "Yes, I know, I know," while we stood together, rocking back and forth in grief. Only grief.

Over the years I have thought often about my experience with Mrs. Warner and her son. Among other things, I wonder about Mark and the gun. What was he waiting for? I ask myself, aware that I will never know the answer. I envision Mark lying in bed, comforted nightly by the fact that he had a way out available to him. I imagine him taking account each night, weighing the toll of his demise against his ability to suffer it. The imbalance could be reconciled by a simple flick of the trigger. But that never happened. At some point, one critical brain neuron gave way to render Mark incapable of negotiating a trigger or recognizing the threshold between life and death.

I also think about the way that grief generally arrives in our lives—in specific or particular forms. Like that of an old woman hobbling on a cane or an anguished man speaking from a dark, interior abyss. Sometimes I bundle all the separate images I remember from the ward into one composite image. But this can be shaken into its parts whenever a new grief arrives.

And then I recall the moments with Mrs. Warner when I felt formless, part of some dark, underground river of grief coursing through each one of us, joining and nourishing us all. One existing beyond and before every one of us, preceding our differentiations into our separate lives, our particular pains as mothers, sons, and physicians. I believe that it was within that realm of shared, primordial grief that Mrs. Warner finally felt located in place with me, both of us recognizing in the other the common stream from which our particular grief flowed. With that recognition she fell into my arms.

Although I'll never know what Mark meant by "books on a map," for myself I imagine the way that each of our seemingly disparate and particular life stories can be mapped always in relationship to one another. Perhaps not in the happenstance of geography or time, or by the particular ways we arrive at one another's doorstep. But certainly within the shared map of our souls. Within this place of grief that opens into each one of us.

Waves

James, a master of several languages, spoke only four words during the entire three months of his hospitalization. He did not apportion his words roughly one per month; rather, he grouped them into a single sentence, which he delivered from the hospital chair to which his limp body had been tethered by soft restraints. Friends had wheeled him to the hospital courtyard so he could attend our annual AIDS Services picnic.

What James said that humid summer day was, "I want a beer."

Amid the blaring brass of the Gay Men's Marching Band, the amplified voices of impassioned speakers at the stage podium, and the boisterous celebration of the energetic crowd, there was no sound more sensational, more moving, more awesome than James's voice.

Several stunned staff members elbowed through the crowd toward James as news of his first spoken words rippled through the gathering. In my astonishment, I smiled and cried at the same confused moment. An educator present at the picnic would later recount this event in her future lectures about AIDS dementia. One of the nurses would adopt "I want a beer," as shorthand to refer to the visitations of the mysterious on our AIDS ward. Three years later I would become partners with a psychotherapist who one night would painfully reconstruct the story of a client named James whose brilliance and liveliness tragically constricted over weeks; whose AIDS dementia had rendered him mute the final months of his life but for four words spoken at an AIDS picnic. One decade later I would meet a writer who, at our first encounter, would reminisce about an intimate friendship she had shared with a man who died from AIDS ten years before, and that his name was James.

James never spoke a word to me during our almost-daily visits throughout his entire hospitalization. He just stared at me, directly and incessantly. His expressionless walnut-brown eyes perfectly tracked me around his room. All the while, his facial expression remained calm, still, and neutral. The nurses had maintained his thick black mustache as a razor-sharp crescent above his strong chin and soft, wide mouth. His constantly peaceful appearance and open, directed gaze were unlike the diverse faces of dementia I had seen previously, faces projecting depression, anger, confusion, agitation, withdrawal, suspicion, irritation, or disinhibition.

Only twice did I see James' expression shift: once, after I threatened to take advantage of him as a captive audience and reveal the entire saga of my "long and sordid life," he laughed; another time, he smiled when I wore bright silver earrings to which he pointed, motioning his desire to touch them. I leaned over the side rails of his bed so he could tap my earrings with his index finger. Our heads very close together, I felt as though I could drop into his soft, open eyes and just float.

In the beginning of our relationship, I rounded with James in the early morning, before his many friends crowded his bedside. After checking his lungs or cleaning his skin ulcers or doctoring him in the usual ways, I sat beside his bed in a faux leather chair and tried to make contact with him.

But his intense, steadfast gaze and absolute quietude unnerved me. Initially, I would flee from the silence and escape into language. Unfortunately, my language often constituted a rather pathetic babbling. Trying to fill up the apparent emptiness between us with more coherent or regulated content, I later began to read him sections of the daily *Oakland Tribune.* He reflected no distinguishing responses to my offerings of hard news, etiquette advice, sports columns, gardening tips, or tasty recipes. Occasionally I worried that he was dismissing or judging me with his seeming passivity and silence.

One chaotic day on the AIDS ward, at the end of James's first month of hospitalization, I forgot to bring the newspaper to our visit. I was too frenzied to take the time needed to climb one flight of stairs to my second-floor office and retrieve it from my briefcase. I considered walking to the visitor's lounge for a paperback substitute, but I feared encountering more opportunity for distraction in the main hallway. So I entered James' room hurriedly and empty-handed.

After touching James' shoulder and greeting him aloud, I sunk down in my usual chair near his bedside. My nerves were firing away like distressed Morse code signals, communicating overload and uncertainty and anxiety. One ward patient was bleeding profusely from his gut, and someone in the intensive-care unit was dying. I decided to use my few minutes with James as a quiet refuge in which I might better think rationally and calmly about these medical urgencies.

My mind raced so quickly that I remained unaffected by James' persistent stare. Throughout the kinetic internal dialogue within my head, I had been looking at James without consciously seeing him. I remained insulated by self-reflection, unaware of any personal activity between us.

While considering my advisement to the family of the desperate young man surviving on rapid blood transfusions, my mind suddenly tired of the racket in my head. Like a theater curtain rising, my mental ramblings lifted to reveal a clear view of James' presence as a part of my own. My gaze penetrated his. Language became distracting noise, a burdensome disturbance. I stopped talking to myself. And I slowly heard the silence, felt it peaceful and expansive between us. I found myself drawn fully into it, into this place where I floated above words, above all the words that had ever been spoken. Above the words *you* and *me*.

From that point on, my morning rounds with James became deeply meditative occasions for me. Sometimes we breathed together, in cadence. If people walked into the room we would turn our heads in unison to acknowledge them, then quickly turn to face each other again.

I often wondered how I was drawn into the pool of James' life without there being any language between us. How I felt my connection to him continue to deepen without the usual offerings of speech to convey thought and dialogue and humor, to illuminate personality and character.

I wondered, too, how the body registered deeply sensed connections with other human beings. And by what circuitry that could bypass language and all that language shaped? Were there subatomic particles that bounced excitedly and made quantum leaps from one person to another, stimulating neurons in specific regions of each other's brains? Were electromagnetic waves responsible, radiating from one heart and lodging in another?

And I thought how, fundamentally, physically, we were actually composed of waves, and how sometimes, inevitably, these waves would flow together as one large body. Our basic nature was waves flowing to and from each other and toward one great sea. This is what I imagine James and I communicated day after day.

Up on the Roof

Teach us to care and not to care.
Teach us to sit still.
—T. S. ELIOT, ASH-WEDNESDAY

Sharon had poked so many needles into her body that, according to basic physical principles, all her insides should have leaked out. She ought to have been made porous, deflated, dependent upon a steady infusion of water and air to sustain her bodily form.

For nineteen of her thirty-two years she had used heroin and supported her habit by prostituting herself in the business district of downtown Oakland. She arrived on our AIDS ward saturated with HIV and racked by spiking fevers. Her skin was a matte of pus and scab and track marks draped over her skeleton. No one, not even Sharon, could find an accessible vein through which we could give her the intravenous antibiotics that she desperately needed. For two days we had been able to use a spindly, miniscule vein on the backside of her thumb before it burst from the physical pressure of the intravenous solution.

The only recourse we had was to insert a central line, an intravenous tubing that would tunnel through the soft, fleshy parts of Sharon's chest until it divined a large vein near the central locale of her heart. I always hesitated to insert these lines into injection drug users since the lines were often abused as an easy portal for surreptitious drug use in the hospital. Users would poke the plastic tubing with their syringes full of heroin or speed, mechanically disrupting the line or introducing infection. Almost always they seemed certain that the medical staff was oblivious to or naive about their subversion.

Not surprisingly, Sharon enthusiastically welcomed the insertion of the central line. Per protocol, the physician proceduralist administered one hundred milligrams of the narcotic Demerol to her as analgesic preparation for the procedure. However, immediately after his introductory poke of the stylet into her neck, Sharon refused to proceed, claiming, "Damn! I can still feel everything. Get me more Demerol."

The frustrated physician looked at me for consultation; I nodded to concur with Sharon's "recommendation," as I thought it likely that her years of drug abuse had rendered her narcotic tolerance rather high. The physician then gave Sharon an additional fifty milligrams. Minutes later, Sharon slurred "Okay, I'm good. Let's go." She looked extremely comfortable.

But, just as the physician positioned the central line correctly into the right side of Sharon's heart, she became unarousable and ceased breathing. The physician ordered emergent delivery of Narcan, a drug employed to neutralize the effects of Demerol, and the assistant nurse rapidly injected one ampule of the antidote through Sharon's tenuous new central line.

Within seconds, much to our relief, Sharon roused and began to breathe spontaneously. However, suddenly she sat upright on the procedure table, yanked the central line out from her neck, and screamed violently and viscerally at the physician, "You mother-fucking asshole! You god damn son of a bitch! I'm gonna kill you bastards!"

With HIV-tainted blood oozing from the puncture wound in her neck, Sharon bolted out of the procedure room and into the hallway, still screaming and cursing. She ran through the AIDS ward exit and into the corridor connecting our ward to the adjacent hospital building. She entered a stairwell and bounded up the steps.

Several staff members and I pursued her up two flights of stairs that led to the roof. Sharon was close to the eaves when we grabbed her and dragged her back into the stairwell. She kicked and bucked while we tried to subdue her. I worried that her blood might splatter on us, and I kept reminding my coworkers to be careful. Finally, with Sharon's wiry arms pinned behind her, I was able to apply a pressure bandage to the hole near her throat.

We dropped into a trembling silence as we restrained Sharon and waited anxiously for the sheriff's deputies to escort her to the county's medical locked-bed facility. While we held her, Sharon continued to spew her venomous rage at us. We were shocked to hear that she was "pissed off" precisely because we had "robbed" her of her Demerol high with the Narcan reversal. She screamed that it would have "served [us] mother fuckers right" had she jumped from the roof. She said she'd like to kill me.

I sat in horror watching her writhe and twitch like a trapped animal, listening to her vile curses. Her primitive interior life exposed in such raw and feral a manner frightened me, showed me a form of human existence that I would have preferred not to know about. Its pure autistic savagery felt like a dark power that could inhabit me, and this haunted me more than her physical threats.

Sharon was still bristling and fuming an hour later when two nervous deputies ushered her away. Her "Rocky Mountain High" tee-shirt was streaked vertically with trails of her blood.

After she left, the staff and I stood looking at one another awhile, not wanting to return to work just yet. We didn't talk much; mostly groans or words like *god* or *Jesus* or *awful* were exchanged.

For a while, Sharon's expletives seemed to echo in the stairwell. A bright red spot of her blood glistened on a bone-white step. I could not shake my memory of her disfigured body writhing on the landing, her cold slit eyes looking directly into mine, incapable of seeing that we were somehow related creatures. That all of us holding her, preventing her from jumping, trying to treat her infection, were connected beyond our potential utility as her source of drugs. I was chilled by her presumption that her jump from the roof would serve precisely to punish me and the staff.

That evening at home I took a long, warm shower and envisioned Sharon's vitriol and murderous gaze washing off the surfaces of my body. I thought of Sharon's skin— her interface with the world—how she had converted it into an impermeable barrier of scar tissue and off-putting pus and how the inability of even her veins to allow connection was telling of her isolation. She had reduced her body to barter for drugs: on the street, on the procedure table, and on the roof. She had become a hollow vessel for heroin.

I have thought of Sharon often in the moment of her violent rousing on the procedure table after her Demerol high had been truncated by the antidote. I imagine the shock of her having to feel something then, to have to rise from the stagnant anesthetic depths of narcotics back to the damaged surface of her small life, the sadness of her body; perhaps, even, to the unfathomable fact that we would run after her and insist on her life.

I still don't fully understand why I ran to the roof after Sharon that day, or why several others, without adequate protection, reached for her bloodied body. She had been a contentious, bitter, toxic, and deceitful presence on the ward. The blood oozing from her neck had posed considerable risk of contagion to those of us who tried to save her. And in the bigger picture, Sharon's life had been muted by her own hands, and she had suggested that her death would pose meaning only to us. Dashing up the stairwell after her, I had wondered why I should care about the life of a person who had no obvious interest in it herself.

I don't know what reflexes are triggered in perilous moments like these to order muscles and bones into action that insists only on the possibility of life for others. It may be neural circuitry that courses through the heart and compels such action. It may be neurotransmission of impulse that derives from platitudes or ethics in the brain which then command our legs and arms, a central directive that no life should end as a splat from a rooftop. And perhaps it's something like the soul that carries us to rooftops, to heights we never imagined, and to connections we never dreamed probable.

All I know is that, for me, it came down to this: pure reflex movement, reaching into life.

An Ordinary Death

And if he moves his dwelling place, his heavens also move
Where'er he goes, and all his neighborhood bewail his loss.
—WILLIAM BLAKE, MILTON

The last thing I expected to hear at our initial meeting was his dying request. When Casey beckoned me to his bedside, his mother standing fifteen feet away, I thought, well, this patient wants to tell me something a doctor should know but a mother shouldn't hear. I expected him to reveal a medical fact or physical complaint that he considered private.

Leaning sideways over Casey's bed rails, I placed my ear against the open end of his hands cupped around his mouth. He whispered, "Please don't let me die in my mother's house. And please don't let me die in front of her."

In that moment, my neck and head were bent forty-five degrees and my eyes focused diagonally upon the faded watercolor reproduction of lilacs that seemed to adorn the walls of every hospital room. I saw Casey's mother as an oblique figure in the periphery of my vision, her smile at this angle appearing exaggerated and strangely uplifted at one corner. The muscular brown chair in the corner balanced itself on two skinny, wooden legs, and Casey's IV pole looked as though it were about to topple over.

I knew my face moved—my lips parted slightly, my eyebrows shifted—when I registered Casey's request, but my disoriented perspective made me uncertain whether or not my reaction had been of sufficient magnitude to betray an expression that Casey's mother might detect and find disturbing or provocative. I marshaled my lips and eyes into strict neutral and straightened up. Most of my life I had been uncomfortable with secrets, especially those told in open view of others. And this particular secret worried me immediately.

"Well," I said, trying to sound composed, "if there's anything you need while you're here, please feel free to tell me or one of the AIDS staff nurses."

Casey's mother replied, "Thank you, we will. I do wonder if you could estimate how long you think Casey will be here?"

Now, with both of us vertical, I could see that her smile was soft and symmetrically configured. I studied her briefly, wondering why her son would wish to be separated from her at the moment of his death. She seemed to be a loving, caring woman who, like many mothers, had made adjustments in her life, her heart, to integrate her son's homosexuality and to provide him care throughout his suffering and death. She exuded a simple elegance in her black corduroys and over-hanging white blouse, and she carried herself with a quiet self-confidence and lack of pretension.

Casey suffered from cryptococcal meningitis, a rampant proliferation of a fungal infection around his brain. He had failed treatment with antifungal therapies elsewhere, and he transferred to our hospital for an aggressive second attempt at control.

"I'm going to guess a week, tops," I replied. "But it could be sooner, depending on the time it takes you to become comfortable hanging the intravenous medications yourself."

"Excellent," she responded confidently. "I'm a fast learner, and we want to get home as soon as possible. Right, Casey?"

Casey turned to face his mother. The two of them looked at each other, smiled, and nodded agreement.

"Oh!" she said suddenly, "I'm supposed to give these medical records to the clerk. Can you direct me?"

I directed her to the nurses' desk and, when I was certain that she had exited the AIDS ward corridor, I asked Casey, "Is there something else you want to tell me? About you and your mom? Is there a problem at home?"

"Oh, no," he answered immediately, his voice thin and fragile. "My mother is really wonderful to me. We love each other a lot. I know she could handle my death, but that's not the issue. I just don't want her with me when I die. I don't want anyone there. I want a quiet, private death. One that's just mine. No interference from anyone. And, please, I don't want my mother to know about this discussion."

I had taken care of other people who had expressed a wish to be alone when they died. Often, this wish seemed to serve a fear, a way of trying to claim a painful aloneness as a choice. Other people believed that they had to protect their loved ones from witnessing some final detail of their dying.

But Casey seemed peaceful and loved, and his wish did not hint at fear or anger or despondency. He was smiling at me, waiting for my response. His direct, simple request to experience his own death in a particular way cleared a mindful of contrary considerations from my head. Like, oh, certainly you'd want your mother there. And your partner. And there's your sister and her kids. And, really, no one should die alone. I can't imagine it for myself...

Those words—"I can't imagine it for myself"—were finally, after many deaths, clear and immediate clues for me, warning me not to assert my personal views or needs. I had attended deaths for several years with varying kinds and degrees of mostly unconscious self-interest. At first, this manifested as my need to save physical life as a way of enacting my physician's skills and "duties." Later, as a need to demonstrate my compassion and fearlessness at the bedsides, to forge and test a certain self-image. Then, wanting to be someone who could help, who was familiar with death, as my unwitting tendency to project my own ideal death upon the death at hand. Finally, as a desire to explore the mysteries of life and death so ripe at the bedsides. It had taken a while, but I realized that the most important thing I could do at the deathbed was to simply get out of the way, to put aside all my concerns about me: how I was performing or providing or behaving or being, how I perceived an ideal death.

"Yes," I replied, "a quiet, private death."

"Thanks," he said relaxing back against his pillow, "I knew you'd understand."

But suddenly I felt disturbed, realizing that there were likely to be formidable obstacles in the way of providing Casey a final solitude. We had just discussed his going home; short of spying on his house and employing a tactical squad to whisk him away to a private room in his final hours, I had no idea how I could really honor Casey's request.

"What's wrong?" Casey asked. "Your forehead looks like an accordion."

"Well, I just realized that I promised you something prematurely. How am I going to get your devoted mother away from you? Especially if you're at her home? I don't know how you can be alone without telling your wish to your mother beforehand."

Casey turned and looked at me with such certainty and calm that I felt disoriented again, in a false perspective of unwarranted doubt and anxiety.

"Just do what you can," he said. "We'll be fine."

"We"? I wondered. How did the two of us suddenly become a *we*?

Before I could say more, Casey's mother returned. From that moment on, she stayed by his side, night and day, and rapidly learned how to administer his medications. Four days later, Casey was ready to be discharged home to the capable care of his mother and a home health nurse.

I thought of Casey frequently during the ensuing weeks of his absence. I wanted to know more about this stranger who had entrusted his wish to me. I found myself wondering what books he liked to read, how he dressed, what made him laugh, who his friends might be. I wanted to know why he looked at me so full of confidence and tranquility in response to my doubts.

I worried that he might die suddenly, within his mother's home, from a sudden drop in blood pressure or a massive seizure. That there would be no time to transfer him to our ward, no real opportunity for me to distract his mother from his bedside. I feared that I would be left forever holding my fragment of his unfulfilled wish.

I phoned Casey's house once, to speak with him, to hear how he was doing. Also, the circumstances of our private negotiation were so mysterious that I wanted a moment of his voice as a reassuring token of his existence. But his mother reported that he was too weak and frail to speak on the phone.

Within one month, the home health team contacted me to arrange for Casey's rehospitalization to initiate intensive intravenous pain management. During the difficult weeks following his discharge, Casey had suffered from progressively debilitating headaches as his meningitis spread and expanded beneath his bony skull. Painful waves of high-pressured infected spinal fluid rolled across his brain, eroding nerve cables and washing away islands of intellect and personality. He had recently decided that he wanted nothing more than comfort care. Large doses of oral narcotics had proved insufficient to dull his suffering, and his awareness flickered through his narcosis with surges of excruciating pain.

We placed Casey in a quiet room with a view of the hospital courtyard and initiated a constant intravenous drip of morphine. Soon, he ceased groaning and wincing and flinching, and his breathing became regular. I had hoped for a private moment with him, but his mother was afraid to leave his side. "I want to be here when he dies," she said.

I made frequent visits to Casey's room, trying to steal a moment alone with him, but I failed consistently. His mother stayed vigilant at his bedside. She slept each night, semi-erect, in the brown Naugahyde recliner wedged into the corner of his room. Every day she and I agreed that Casey looked comfortable.

On the third day of his hospitalization, Casey slipped into a coma. I despaired then that he and I would ever discuss and reconcile his problematic wish. And, on the fifth day, Casey's mother announced that she was looking forward to a consultation with community hospice representatives so that arrangements could be made to return Casey home for terminal care. My heart plummeted to my feet.

I don't really understand what happened next, but, perhaps an hour after her announcement, I rose suddenly from my chair at another patient's bedside and walked to Casey's room. I saw then that Casey's mother was gone. I went to the veranda from which I observed her crossing the parking lot toward the hospital cafeteria.

I returned to Casey's bedside. His wasted body lay flaccid in the buttery sunlight of a warm spring day that filtered through his window. I stroked his feverish head and held one of his limp hands. Then I bent forward, bringing my mouth close to his ear, and whispered, "Casey, it's me, Kate." He remained completely still.

I continued to hold his hand. I pushed one his corkscrew curls from his damp forehead back toward his pillow. The longer I looked at him, the more familiar he seemed to become. His thin angled nose and dark coiled hair mirrored those of my younger brother's. His squared cheekbones belonged to an old professor. His lifeless body reminded me of scores of young men in war-scene photographs from the newspapers. It began to seem as though I were holding a hand connected to all these other people.

I leaned toward him again, I told him I loved him, and I whispered, "Your mother left for a little while. So you can go now, if that's still what you want to do. You can go."

Immediately, without pause, Casey drew one deep breath, and, after releasing it, he died.

I stood still, stunned. I didn't believe what had happened. I thought that I had imagined it. I assessed Casey for a pulse and found none. Had he really been waiting for my signal? Had he actually decided when to die?

In the absence of his breathing, Casey's room became impossibly quiet. I looked around at the chipped, green paint on the walls and the wrinkled, yellowed linoleum floor, all of which suggested that this was not a place the extraordinary would visit.

Then I thought of Casey's face the day we had spoken privately; his vivid expression of clarity and faith had been unwavering. I began to look around the room again, imagining it through his calm and certain vision, and the mysteriousness of his death simply insisted. I was able to accept that Casey had died in this room, with me, in this incredible, ineffable manner. That, knowing so little of each other in the usual personal ways, Casey had trusted me as sentry to the occasion of his death, and I had known what to do, trusting the unseen strings that pulled me gently into his final moments.

I continued to hold Casey's hand, not wanting to let him go. I wanted to hold him, hold everything, until I fully grasped what had happened. If I could not understand the experience intellectually, I wanted something to happen that would certify the imponderability of it—a celestial murmur, a bright light, or a shadowy image of a god projected on the walls.

But all I heard was silence, which quickly yielded to the clanking of an IV pole in the hallway and a blue jay's squawk in the cypress outside. All I saw was Casey's body silhouetted against the window framing the courtyard, where patients sat on wood benches and smoked cigarettes, where disorderly rows of crimson salvia moved in a gentle breeze. An empty Cheetos bag tumbled across the lawn.

I looked at our hands, still held together against the white cotton sheets. Soon my incomprehension gave way to wonder. I released Casey's hand, and I waited as its warmth lifted from the surface of my palm. Into the room about us, through the window, and into the courtyard. As ordinary as breath, as routine as a spring day.

The Soap Opera Within

O my body! I dare not desert the likes of you
in other men and women,
nor the likes of the parts of you.
I believe that the likes of you are to stand or fall
with the likes of the soul
(and that they are the soul).
I believe that the likes of you shall stand or fall with my poems,
and that they are my poems,
Man's, woman's, child's, youth's, wife's,
husband's, mother's, father's,
young man's, young woman's poems…
—WALT WHITMAN, SONG OF MYSELF

The Apocryphon of John states that a total of 365 angels labored on the human until "limb by limb, the psychic and material body was finished." While not wishing to refute sacred doctrine, I would have to say that my experience on the AIDS ward has led me to believe that many more laborers—more angels than could dance on the head of a pin—were involved in our complex creation. And the infinite variation in our human forms leads me to suspect that the worker angels either lacked, or, I prefer to think, devilishly rejected, a standard template; they also seem to have enjoyed a substantial amount of creative freedom.

From the beginning of the epidemic, AIDS has provided us with a unique lens through which we can view the "psychic and material" bodies of both individuals and society. It has brought into closer view the psychology of individuals facing death and the complex psychology of a society struggling to understand and contain a new epidemic. It has directed our medical attention to the devastating biologic impact of a submicroscopic virus on the lives of millions of affected individuals, and it has shown us the tremendous material toll that epidemics can exact on a society and its culture.

Focusing this lens specifically on human sexuality showcases the angels' imaginative handicraft. Among the patients on our AIDS ward, there existed a remarkable array of genders, sexualities, and sexual practices—stunning compositions and permutations that were decidedly more prevalent here than among other populations of patients. There were men who had sex with other men and referred to themselves as "straight" because they were also traditionally married or because they distinguished their sexual practices from their sexual identity. There were women who prostituted to men who called themselves "lesbian" because they differentiated sex acts from desire and sexuality. There were men who dressed as women who might identify as heterosexual, homosexual, bisexual, or asexual. There were men who called themselves women. Men in hormonal or surgical transitions to becoming a biologic woman who might then adopt the identity of lesbian. There was bisexuality and even straight-out heterosexuality.

For me, always, focused in the center of the lens is Edie.

Edie was a thirty-one-year-old, African American, biologic male with AIDS; she was homeless, impoverished, transsexual, and addicted to drugs and alcohol. In her medical chart, her demographics were blandly recorded as: "31-yo, AA, M, Trans, IDU, ETOH."

"Hello, honey," she greeted me at our first meeting. She lay in bed, dressed in a shiny red nightgown and matching robe. Sweat beaded her forehead, pearls beaded her neck. She was breathing rapidly, ostensibly short of breath.

"Oh, you know my name," I replied.

She laughed and responded, "Yes, and now I got your number, too."

I had already reviewed Edie's medical record and the chest X-ray obtained by the emergency room physician. Odds were extremely high that Edie had the "AIDS pneumonia," pneumocystis.

"How would you like me to address you?" I asked.

"Well, 'Queen' would be nice," she responded.

" 'He' queen or 'she' queen?" I asked, having learned through a prior faux pas that some transsexuals preferred the safety of the male pronoun while within the uncertain psychosocial environment of the hospital.

Edie studied her plum-painted fingernails a moment before answering, " 'She' will do."

" 'She' it is," I said. "Do you mind if I examine you before we review your test results?"

"I'm all yours," Edie replied, extending her arms weakly but elegantly across the bed.

To examine the swollen lymph nodes in her neck, I pushed aside Edie's shoulder-length hair, noting it to be at least six inches longer than mine. To inspect for oral fungus or viral infections, I asked Edie to open her ruby-red painted lips, acknowledging that I myself never applied makeup. When I placed my stethoscope to Edie's chest, I saw that her estrogen-fed breasts were larger than mine. When I listened to her heart, I heard sounds that were the same as my own.

"Edie," I said, "I'm not sure how much the ER doctors told you, but it looks like you've got..."

"AIDS," she blurted out. "Yes, I already know." She placed one hand across her chest and shook her downcast head, saying, "I already know."

"I'm very sorry, Edie," I said. "That's probably true."

"Well, I'm not surprised in the least," she said. "Y' know, each of us is just waiting for it to happen. It comes to visit us all sooner or later. It's simply my turn, I suppose."

"We've got very effective antibiotics for your pneumonia," I offered.

"I'm relieved," Edie replied. "I mean, about knowing I got the AIDS. Now I won't have to worry about all my strange aches and pains. They got a name—AIDS."

Relief was not an uncommon initial response to a formal diagnosis of AIDS; many men and women who engaged in at-risk activities found their anticipatory anxiety finally quelled by the realization of their great fear. But after diagnosis, in the mid-eighties, life was measured in months. I wondered if she was afraid as well as relieved.

"Edie," I said, "what other kinds of responses do you have?"

"Well, I'm feeling very disappointed," she replied soberly before falling silent.

"Yes, AIDS is hard, and..." I began slowly.

"No, no, no," she interrupted, waving her big hand. "No. I'm disappointed because this means that I'll never get my surgery. Now no one will do it if I have AIDS."

Edie had already availed herself of female sex hormones in a years-long preparation for transsexual surgery, and the fullness of her breasts and the softness of her belly reflected their influences on her body. Still, she spoke with that airy, husky voice that resonated with testosterone's lingering presence, and her parodically exaggerated feminine mannerisms were a clear giveaway that her chromosomes were XY.

"Oh, yes, of course," I replied, mentally reassigning our discussion priorities. "You've been waiting long?"

"All my life," she said sadly. "I almost had enough saved last year, but with Darryl's problems and all, the money went fast."

"Darryl?" I asked.

"My boyfriend, Darryl," Edie explained, coughing delicately.

"Does he know you're here? That you're sick?"

"No, he had a serious problem with the pipe. Last year he took all my money and ran from the police. I don't know where he is."

"I'm sorry, Edie," I replied. I took a Kleenex and blotted a streak of mascara that had trailed with a tear down her cheek. "Do you have other support? Family?"

She started to cry even harder now. "No," she managed. "At least no one who'll admit being family."

I was becoming increasingly depressed by Edie's situation, which seemed to expand into new territories of despair every time I asked a question. Her suffering was formidable and expansive, and my own heart was expanding in response. I didn't want to provoke more sadness, for her or me, so I said, "We'll take good care of you, Edie. The antibiotics should be up soon, it's dinner time, and the social worker will see you in the morning. I'm here for anything you might need."

After a few deep, calming sighs, Edie said: "Doctor Honey, I just want to be sure that I'll get my hormones tonight. I've taken them for five years." She pulled an empty prescription bottle from one of her black plastic garbage bags.

"These pills have saved my life," she continued. "My inside life as well as my outside one."

"How have these changed you internally?" I asked.

"Oh," she replied, "they dulled the male hormones and let me get to the business of being a woman. I used to be very unhappy before Dr. Lindsay prescribed these. I tried to kill myself once. In fact, I stopped shooting speed, almost completely, since I been on them. Can't say I gave up alcohol, though."

"Estrogen sounds like a miracle drug," I said.

"Better'n speed!" Edie replied.

The next morning I found Edie in the hallway, leaning heavily against her IV pole, in a weak but spirited argument with another patient. "Hey, what's going on?" I asked.

"Gay men think they *own* AIDS," Edie scowled.

The other patient interjected, "This *person* here says that gay men have all the AIDS money, and that they're not spreading it around to women. Like it's weird, 'cuz I know he's…"

"She's going back into her room with me now," I interrupted.

I escorted Edie into her room, and, after untangling her IV lines, plugging her IV monitor back into the electrical socket, and redistributing her blankets to her expressed preferences so as to leave her rather large feet exposed, I stood beside her and asked what had happened.

"Gay men," she bristled.

"Edie," I said, "I don't understand. Haven't all your sexual partners been men?"

"Of course they've all been; but they've all been *straight* men," she replied matter-of-factly.

"Oh," I faltered. "So you've never considered yourself a gay man—ever?" I asked.

The rolling of Edie's eyes sufficed for an answer.

While I was confused by Edie's statements, I decided that it was too much for her, particularly in the midst of the current upset, to explain them to me. I nodded my head, checked Edie's congested wheezing lungs, and we discussed more of the medical facts of AIDS.

Intermittently throughout the day, whenever I tried to understand Edie's position on gender and sexuality, my mind felt thinned, like it had been stretched too far. However, once I realized that Edie had completely separated gender from sexuality, in complex permutations, I understood that Edie and Darryl considered themselves a heterosexual couple.

On the third day of her hospitalization, Edie "confessed" that she had been taking double or triple doses of hormones to accelerate her femininization "before I die." Then she started to cry, her face struggled with a pained expression, and she finally blurted out, "Oh, Doctor Scannell, I want the surgery so bad." All her flamboyance and bravado had dissolved.

The havoc inflicted on Edie's body by the AIDS virus seemed to pale in comparison to the greater suffering of Edie's flesh and soul that was born of an anguishing dissonance between her male biology and her contrary experience of being gendered a female. It seemed such a primal agonizing schism. A maddening entrapment within a biologic mistake.

"The hormones aren't enough, are they?" I asked.

"No," she replied, wiping her nose and coughing. "In fact, they sometimes make you realize even more that you want the real body that goes with them."

I wished that I had something to soothe Edie's despair; I felt so inadequate with my little parcel of antibiotics. But I began to wonder if even surgery could help her. Could you create a woman with a recipe, a chemical here and a body part there? What had happened with the connective tissues between Edie's "psychic and material" bodies? What were those 365 angels up to when they created Edie?

I placed my hand on Edie's shoulder, and she grasped it in hers.

"If there were some way I could make you feel better about that, I would," I said. "Would you like to see a counselor? I can contact one from the transsexual-transgender support services in San Francisco."

When Edie declined my offer—"I've done all that more times than I can count"—I was secretly relieved. The last time I had contacted someone from that group to provide educational inservice on sex and gender issues for our medical and nursing staff, I had to defend my decision to decline a date with that spokesperson. My "no, thank you," was challenged as homophobic and heterophobic and even "biophobic."

By day four, Edie's pneumonia had improved remarkably, and we discussed switching from intravenous to oral antibiotics. Although Edie's medical progress was gratifying, her improvement raised the issue of imminent hospital discharge. I winced considering Edie's return to the streets; the social workers had yet to locate community housing for her. I offered to bring Edie some of my clothes from home.

She placed her hand over her mouth and laughed. "Doctor Honey, that's so sweet of you! Really. But, well, your clothes aren't quite feminine enough for me." Edie then proceeded to discuss, with dramatic flare, the kinds of gowns and heels and jewelry that she might find acceptable. There were "standards that had to be met," she explained. She was not going to live her last days "looking like *What Ever Happened to Baby Jane*."

I had always been annoyed by some men's high-camp versions of femininity. I found their parodies of women— as brainless monsters of fashion or bitchy gossipy castrators—misogynist and aggressive. These parodies also seemed defensive, acting out some of men's greatest fears about the nature of women. Simultaneously, because they were so obviously unauthentic, they provided a way for the high-camper to make it obvious that he retained the powers of being masculine.

Edie's dire circumstances pushed my reactions further. She aspired to a notion of feminine behavior that I had never witnessed in any biologic female; and she wanted surgery to concretize it. What was this unauthentic femininity about, really? And wasn't concretizing this parodical feminine persona—this masculine construct— paradoxically "embodying" the masculine after all?

And how was it that Edie knew what a woman was when most of the biologic women I knew didn't fully understand what that meant?

"Edie," I said, "perhaps I'll pick up some fashion tips from you later. But..."

"Yes," she said, "you'd look great with some color in your cheeks and even a little eyeliner, not much, maybe…"

I put my hands around my head and pretended to scream. "You're making me crazy!" I said.

She laughed, "So it *is* contagious."

"Apparently so," I replied.

Then, after looking at me tenderly, Edie said: "You know, Doctor Scannell, I miss my girlfriends so much."

I was lagging behind in my morning rounds, to say nothing of my comprehension, so I hesitated to ask about her "girlfriends."

"Yes, well," I began clumsily.

Then, sadly: "You know, doctor, I wanted my surgery so I could be a lesbian. Now I'll never know what that's like."

After working on the AIDS ward for several years, I was rarely stunned by anyone's sexual story. But Edie's comment disoriented me again. "Yes, well, that seems… likely," I returned lamely.

After an evening of bewildered preoccupation trying to understand the permutations of Edie's gender identity and sexuality, I decided to bring my koan to her for direct enlightenment. The next morning, I found her in bed studying her face in a red plastic hand mirror, plucking black commas of wiry hairs from her dimpled chin. A ragged paperback copy of *Death of a Salesman* lay on her lap.

"Edie," I said, "forgive me, but…I wonder if you could help me understand all the vice-versa of your sexuality? I just want to know what you're going through."

Edie looked at me with great affection, and her stubbled face softened thoroughly. She looked truly, if strangely, maternal. "You do, don't you?" she asked.

After I nodded, Edie sighed deeply and patted the bed to invite me to sit. "Well, girlfriend," she began, "you see, I'm a lesbian 'at heart.' You know, emotionally. Nothing beats emotional intimacy between two women. See what I'm saying?"

I was unprepared for her explanation, but I gamely replied, "I can understand that." Then, remembering that all her sexual relationships had been exclusively with men, I asked, "But do you believe that surgery would change your sexual desire—to include women, too?"

"Oh, no," Edie replied. "My body wants sex with men only. When it comes down to the wild thing, well...there's no substitute for a man. Gotta have it with an m-a-n," she spelled.

I was stymied by the mind-bending notion that a biologic male with exclusive sexual preferences for men considered himself heterosexual and a woman, and would become surgically transgendered to a cartoonish female persona so as to identify as a lesbian who did not have sex with women.

Through my own felt experience, I could understand the wide range of Edie's interior life; I believed that Tiresias, the mythic figure with fluid gender and sexuality, roamed inside each of us and was actually a module routinely installed by those angels. But there seemed to be something fractured about Edie's spectrum of internal experience. Hers did not flow like a seamless, fluid continuity of sexuality, one that could shift internally, painlessly, regardless of the particular physical body it inhabited. Her multifaceted identities seemed to be composed of discontinuous, individual ones. There was a maleness she wished to surgically amputate, an exaggerated femininity to be concretized by chemicals and surgical reconstruction, and rigid separations between gender and sexuality and sexual practice. Her pain was the most telling of the fractures.

"Edie, I wonder if surgery would have ever been enough for you?" I said. "I mean, even if you had it, wouldn't you suffer from being *just* a woman? What about your desire for the other men who've wanted you in the way you are now?"

"Well," Edie replied, "I'm not sure. I tried to figure all that stuff out by accessorizing for years. You know, with little—and, oh, sometimes very *big*—goodies from that shop on Valencia Street. And I'm here to say that rubber, or whatever that stuff is, is just not real enough to know."

"But I'm thinking about how sexuality can be independent, at least sometimes, of particular organs or accessories," I said.

"Yes," Edie replied, "but sex without them is like music without an orchestra to play it. You know, on paper you can imagine how beautiful the music sounds, but, with an orchestra, you can actually feel the music. My motto is, Play that music! Play, and let's dance!" She slumped down in bed, laughing, obviously pleased with herself.

"Edie," I remarked, "You amaze me. The possibilities of you seem endless."

"Multiple personalities?" she said in mock horror.

"No," I replied, "it's more like there's a grand, romantic epic within you. You know—the man in you could court the woman in you who could be having an affair with the lesbian in you who is pregnant with the turkey-baster child of the gay man in you…"

"Oh!" she exclaimed, "you got that right, girlfriend! A little *Peyton Place!* No wonder I'm so tired all the time!"

We created other outrageous plots. Edie brainstormed further characters "lurking inside" who wanted to be included: an evil twin sister and a young, romantic schoolboy were her favorites. We incorporated them into various scenes. Edie's laugh was a wondrous mix of sound, a practiced feminine giggling alternating with a deep, baritone belly laugh. When she tossed her head back, slapping her hands on the bed, her red wig shifted backward a little, but she didn't seem to care.

Finally, Edie sighed and, with downcast eyes and lowered voice, she said, "Yes, indeed, a soap opera. We'll call my life *As the World Turns to the Last Days of My Life. Really.*"

I looked at Edie, aware that I might never see her again after her hospital discharge in the morning. I thought about how her immutable lifelong suffering was, poignantly, going to end soon at the hand of AIDS. That she might never experience a peaceful sense of a unified self felt heartbreaking. I wished that I could have helped her find the glue, the painless connective tissue, to mend the dualities of her flesh and spirit. I wondered what made Edie suffer from her expansiveness while others sang of its joys. Why some people experienced the spaciousness of being human as a soap opera, while others could live it as a poem.

The Death Certificate

If you do not tell the truth about yourself, you cannot tell it
about other people.

—Virginia Woolf, The Moment and Other Essays

Stephen, like so many other gay men fleeing isolation and discrimination in suburban and rural towns, had migrated to San Francisco in the mid 1970s seeking community. The home he left the day he turned eighteen was a rambling, white three-story house on fifty acres of prime Missouri farmland. For two years he had prepared his mother for his departure, explaining his need to live in an urban area where people were less likely to judge and ostracize him because of his homosexuality. His mother understood his suffering and supported his move. Although neither Stephen nor his mother discussed these things with Stephen's father, they each suspected that he was aware of them; this conspiracy of silence prevailed until the time, ten years later, when Stephen lay dying in a AIDS ward bed in San Leandro, California.

Stephen was twenty-eight years old. Already he was an old man, with a hobbled walk, dimmed vision, mild forgetfulness, and a shiny bald head. He was transferred to our ward for terminal care. During the previous three years he had suffered multiple complications of AIDS, including skin cancer with Kaposi's sarcoma, a brain infection with toxoplasmosis, partial blindness from a viral infection of his eyes, pneumonia caused by pneumocystis, and profound weakness and wasting away of his body.

The day I met Stephen, he was crying. He was afraid of his new environment, far from Missouri, far from his neighborhood in San Francisco; he wanted to go home.

"You mean back to San Francisco?" I asked.

"No," he replied, "to my home in Middleton, Missouri."

I knew that in two days, Stephen's mother, Mrs. Saddler, would be visiting from Missouri. The referring physician told me that she had been a very supportive participant in Stephen's care, making as many trips to San Francisco as her job had allowed.

"Stephen," I said, "your mother will be here in a couple of days. Have you discussed going home with her before?"

"No," he managed through his tears. "There's no discussion. She just can't take me."

"Why?" I asked.

He just turned away, crying harder.

I didn't know the particulars of Stephen's understanding with his mother. But many times before, I had witnessed the dramatic, confusing strain on the relationships between gay sons and their parents when AIDS triangulated them. AIDS had the power to either break or mend a troubled relationship. Also, many gay men with terminal illness were convinced that they could not die in their hometowns without having to deal with the imposed burdens of that community's prejudice against homosexuality and AIDS. In addition, the hysteria and fear of AIDS rampant in many AIDS-naive communities often created a hostile environment that intimidated families into not receiving their dying children.

On Stephen's third day of hospitalization, Mrs. Saddler knocked on my office door. I invited her in and offered her coffee. Her skin was clear and solidly white, like porcelain. Her copper hair cascaded to her shoulders in soft curls, and she wore a pastel blue polyester pants suit.

After we exchanged a few pleasantries, Mrs. Saddler cleared her throat and said, "Dr. Scannell, my son has it in his head that he could be returning home with me. I have tried to explain all along that that's not possible. It pains me terribly to see him alone here, dying. It kills me. I try to come as often as I can. But there's no way I can take him home. I mean, we're from a place that's never seen AIDS. And no one there even knows about Stephen being gay. Even his father's never mentioned the word."

The pain experienced by Stephen and his mother seemed stretched beyond tolerance; sociocultural prejudices were pulling on them, ruthlessly aggravating their private grief. As mother and son, they felt they had no place in their home or in their community in which they could love each other now. My heart ached for them both.

"Mrs. Saddler," I replied, "we'll take good care of Stephen while he's here. We have a wonderful group of nurses and an excess of hospital volunteers who can help. If there's any way that you think I could help—even some educational materials for your community…"

"No, no," she interrupted, blotting her nose with a Kleenex. "It's just not worth the pain for Stephen, or the suffering it would cause my husband."

Several days after returning to Missouri, Mrs. Saddler sent me a letter. The postage stamp bore a picture of the American flag. She wrote about the "nice visit" she had had at our hospital and with her son. She felt that Stephen was "in loving hands," and that comforted her greatly. Then she wrote,

> I hope you don't think badly of me for this, but I'd like to ask that you don't mention the word *AIDS* on Stephen's death certificate. We live in a tiny rural community, and there has been no one to our knowledge, even in our county, who has had AIDS. While we are not ashamed of Stephen, and never have been, and never will be, we are concerned that when people here remember him, they remember Stephen for his great school accomplishments (a baseball star, music student, debate team captain, etc.) and not simply that he died with a horrible disease. He's held in such high regard here, but some people are ignorant (not knowingly, but because Missouri is just not like California—re: AIDS) and just wouldn't understand.

She also explained that, because her town was so small and insular, Stephen's death certificate would be seen by people working at the courthouse who would channel the information through the community by word of mouth.

I placed Mrs. Saddler's letter on my desk where it lay face up, seemingly staring at me. I didn't know how to respond. In the early days of the AIDS epidemic, physicians occasionally complied with such requests from family members, contributing to an unquantifiable degree of underreporting of AIDS-related deaths. In 1987, the year Mrs. Saddler's letter was written, media attention to this phenomenon had been provoked after it was disclosed that "AIDS" was intentionally omitted from the death certificate of a famous entertainer (Liberace); prior to a coroner's investigation that verified Liberace's AIDS, the entertainer's manager had remained indignant, declaring it a "vicious rumor" to accuse his client of having the disease.

Mrs. Saddler's plea was not the first one I had personally encountered. On several previous occasions other families of AIDS patients had asked me to exclude AIDS from their son's or daughter's death certificate; but, always, allowing those families to vent their conflicted feelings enabled them to become resigned to its official inclusion.

While sorting through my paperwork, I continued to feel distracted by Mrs. Saddler's letter. Initially, I wondered if her request might be reasonable and right-minded. After all, it would cause no one any material harm if I failed to mention AIDS on Stephen's impending death certificate. Certainly such an omission would not alter the critical fact of Stephen's death. And it would allow his mother to share her grief openly with members of her tight-knit community.

Yet something made me waver. Something blurred, unnamed. I knew only that my hesitation was rooted in my images of Stephen: gasping for air during his pneumonia, moaning in pain, despairing over his impending death from AIDS, suffering the awful distance between his hospital bed and a family hundreds of miles away.

At one point I nearly convinced myself to document only "pneumonia" as the official and singular cause of

Stephen's death. It would be a factual and truthful declaration, since pneumonia would be the decisive mortal blow. Still, not documenting evidence of Stephen's other struggles made me very uncomfortable.

Throughout the remainder of the week, my nagging ambivalence prevailed. As the weekend approached and the specter of Stephen's death loomed larger, I became increasingly disturbed by my dilemma.

That Saturday night I attended a friend's dinner party. Several people, mostly strangers to me, were seated at the table. I felt awkward and uncomfortable as the customary small talk began, and I ascribed this to my general incompetence in such situations. Throughout the ensuing interminable six-course meal, I became incrementally anxious, ill at ease, and restive as the small talk evolved into the wider arena of social and political commentary that seemed to serve the purpose of affirming the unity of the small group at the table and their superior views. I did not share the majority of their ideologic perspectives. I also belonged to some of the demographic groups that they considered inferior or defective.

I would like to say that I registered a dramatic protest and made myself a visible presence that insisted on the legitimacy of my own life. But that is not what happened. Instead, I withdrew into a protective silence and I became vaporlike; the people at the table could not judge or criticize me if I was unseen. So I instructed myself to behave politely and agreeably at the table, to listen quietly and attentively to distasteful conversation and opinions.

By Sunday I had become deeply agitated. I was engaged in an internal dialogue highly critical of my behavior at the dinner, chastising myself for my silence and genteel invisibility. For not having said this or that to contradict the people around me. For not disagreeing with their disagreeable perceptions and opinions. Essentially, I was disturbed that I had rendered myself nonexistent by default, through the sad fact of my self-annihilative silence. I was angry with myself for allowing the truth of who I was to recede behind the popular mythology at the table. It was awful enough to feel the antagonism and aversion of a group of people, but my tormenting regret about my own unwitting cooperation with their venture disturbed me even more.

On Monday morning I finally understood what I had to do about Stephen's death certificate. In the afternoon, I phoned Stephen's mother in Missouri, and we chatted briefly before I updated her about Stephen's rapidly deteriorating condition. I took a deep breath and told her that I had considered her request at great length. "But," I said, "I've realized that I have to write 'AIDS' on your son's death certificate."

I explained that my decision was more than a lawful consideration. I said that I would be making the mistake of rendering Stephen's courageous and exhaustive struggles with AIDS invisible by willfully omitting the word from his certificate. I said that it felt wrong for me to contribute to a silence about Stephen's life by concealing his homosexuality, which might be inferred from an AIDS diagnosis. That I had realized the need to honor the integrity of Stephen's life, and that I would not try to make it look nice or invisible for the needs or convenience of others. I told her that I could not collapse the life Stephen lived with his AIDS diagnosis the three years before he died. I said I was sorry for any inconvenience or difficulty this might cause her in her community. I also expressed my wish that the people of her hometown, once made aware of Stephen's story, would actually come to understand AIDS and homosexuality differently because of their prior relationships with Stephen.

Mrs. Saddler remained silent for a while. Then she said, "I understand. I really do. And, actually I agree with you in most ways. But," she continued, "I'm the one who has to live here, and I'm afraid for Stephen's reputation. My husband just had a stroke, and the commotion in town could upset him seriously. I couldn't stand to lose him now, not right after losing my son."

Together we arrived at a silence on the phone. I thought I could feel her awful uncertainty and dread, like that of a mother viewing her child in the middle of a road with a car fast approaching, tragedy threatening; she was truly powerless to direct the path of her community to their understanding of Stephen's death from AIDS. She would have to stand aside, helpless, and wait for the unpredictable impact upon her son's memory and reputation.

Stephen died six days after our phone conversation. I documented "Pneumonia, due to AIDS" as the official cause of death on his certificate.

One month passed, and I received another letter from Mrs. Saddler. She wrote that a large congregation had attended Stephen's memorial services and that everyone appeared to accept Stephen's death with great compassion and sorrow. That she watched expectantly for some show of disdain for his homosexuality and his illness, but she witnessed none. Old classmates and teachers and employers came to his service, and the minister delivered a beautiful eulogy. She relayed that it was amazing for her to be within her own community for the first time with its members aware of her son's homosexuality, something concealed from them all of Stephen's life. She wrote, "It was wonderful to have Stephen here with me, fully, at last."

During the years that have passed since Stephen's death, when I think of him and his mother I think of the way that one person's life—one person's story—can enlarge the hearts of others, even of an entire community. I also sometimes imagine the way I probably looked sitting at the dinner table that awful night at my friend's home; I still wince at that image and feel grief for all the time I've lost being invisible in my life.

And sometimes I envision a long, expanded table where I sit with Stephen and his mother and a small rural community and my friend's dinner guests. We are feasting on one another's real stories. On the powers of ordinary personal truths to shape a glorious banquet, to nourish a wider human truth.

Exorcises

When we remember that we are all mad,
the mysteries disappear and life stands explained.
—MARK TWAIN, NOTEBOOK

My approach to Tony's room seemed ordinary enough. It was seven in the morning, the usual time I met patients who had been admitted to the ward the previous night. I held a Styrofoam cup brimming with industrial-strength coffee in one hand and Tony's bulky medical records in the other.

Tony's admission note had been brief, because he had refused to speak with the night-call physician or allow a physical examination. The voluminous records accompanying him from the transferring hospital facility stated that Tony suffered from AIDS dementia; he had been "disabled by his agitated depression and paranoid ideations," and he was "unsafe to remain independent at home."

Crossing the threshold of Tony's doorway that morning, I left the ordinary behind and abruptly entered the extraordinary. Nearly naked, Tony stood at the portal, highly agitated, repeating "Shit! Phhht!" I almost ran into him. Startled, I gasped and clumsily managed, "Oh! Yes. Hello! You must be…"

Tony dispensed with the usual greetings. Immediately, he roared—literally roared, "Gur-raaaaaah!"—like a wild lion.

I placed my coffee cup on the table, afraid that either my shaking or his commotion might cause it to spill. Then Tony bellowed, "I DO NOT HAVE AIDS!"

Two alarmed nurses appeared at the door. I indicated that their help was not needed. As they turned away, Tony pulled me to the foot of his hospital bed. He dropped to the ground where he proceeded to perform push-ups, counting after each one: "One, I don't have AIDS; two, I don't have AIDS, three I don't have AIDS..." He repeated this forty times.

I was truly shaken by this exciting introduction to Tony. I watched in awe as he completed all forty reps. Then he sprung up, stood before me, and, with his arms held open, he declared, "See, I'm fine, you bastards!" After that, in alternate English and Italian, he blared a succession of curses against anyone associated with his health care, including me.

"Most people just say, 'Nice to meet you, too,' " I said.

"Damn!" he screamed.

He crouched on the floor in a sprinter's position. He yelled, "Fuck everybody!" as the caustic verbal semaphore signaling a flurry of sprints; he ran circles around me, shouting, "I don't have fucking AIDS!" over and over again with each lap.

Situated in the center of this agitated man's anger and unpredictable behavior, I felt increasingly anxious and vulnerable. I inched back toward his doorway, pulling his furious path with me, trying to get closer to an escape into the hallway. But before I could reach safe ground, Tony stopped his circular sprinting and ran to the corner of his room where he lifted a bulky recliner and began pressing it above his head like a set of iron weights. With each upward thrust he forcefully uttered one word from the sequence, "I—don't—have—it!"

I realized that, throughout my medical career, I had been exposed to many different styles of patients' denial mechanisms, such as the nonchalant woman with the six-inch tumor in her breast who had finally decided to see a doctor; the stoic man with crushing chest pain who would not cease mowing his lawn until all three acres were neatly groomed; the noncompliant diabetic with the frequent-buyer bakery card in his front shirt pocket. But never before had I witnessed anything even remotely resembling Tony's amazing demonstration.

If only force of will had the power to exorcise the AIDS virus, I thought. My heart ached as I watched Tony in his desperation, knowing that his fevered calisthenics were exercises in futility.

I doubted that we'd be able to communicate and, certainly, I was not about to use the word *AIDS* in any discussion with him. Between Tony's agitation and my fear, I thought that there was no room for us to meet. It didn't seem possible to break through his paranoia to reach his ostensible suffering.

Tony's unfocused anger and frustration and violence ricocheted off the walls, without any specific aim; and I worried that he might soon designate me as his target because of the simple happenstance of my presence in his room or my role as his new physician. The unpredictability of his behavior and his frenetic and impossible pace kept me out of sync with him.

While despairing about my situation, I saw Tony suddenly perform a perfect cartwheel across the linoleum floor. Unfortunately, his hospital bed interfered, and he crashed against it. "Tony!" I exclaimed, bending toward him, helping him to his feet, "why don't you…"

But before I could articulate my verb, Tony leapt to his feet and successfully negotiated his cartwheel in the opposite direction, toward his closet. When he concluded, he stood tall and erect, arms akimbo, and claimed proudly, defiantly, "See! I don't have it! How many people with AIDS do *you* know who can do all this?"

After pausing a brief and uncertain moment, I replied, "Well, you are definitely the only one I know."

"Shit," he said, shaking his head. "This is proof. I ain't got the damn thing!" Then Tony lowered his head, scowling and grimacing, repeating "shit," over and over again.

Existential stalemate, parallel planes, magnetically opposed realities, Tony and me. I concluded that it remained completely futile to hope for a place of convergence where we might meet and agree on—well, anything. I decided to leave.

However, just as I motioned a parting gesture with my hand, one corner of my mouth rose and, soon, an irrepressible grin followed. I felt somewhat embarrassed by this, since I did not think it terribly appropriate to the occasion of a difficult patient-physician visit. I tried to suppress my spontaneous grin by tugging my lips downward with my fingers and dramatically furrowing my brows.

But Tony had detected my expression. "What? What the hell?" he inquired.

I realized that my fear of him was dissipating and I felt it yield to a kind of awe. I said, "I was just thinking how, nowadays, we have gentler ways of testing for HIV."

Tony scrutinized me for a moment before plopping himself on the floor and massaging the sore place on his calf that had met his bed. I put my hand on his sweaty shoulder and said, "That was a great cartwheel."

He looked up at me, squinting his cinnamon-brown eyes, flaring his nostrils slightly, waiting. I had not yet controlled my rather mindless grin, which, to my dismay, was broadening. I bit the inside of my cheeks trying to create a painful distraction.

But I was experiencing joy. A calm, vernacular joy that entered the small, dull hospital room in which Tony and I had rebounded off each other. I was dazzled with gratitude for having been allowed to witness such a remarkably unique and genuine expression of life.

My heart took the lead and made me understand then that part of Tony's distress was his fear that his dementia had insulated him. Like so many people with AIDS dementia, he no longer possessed confidence about his intellect, trust in his sanity, and control of his emotions. Human relationships were precarious, uncertain propositions. Judgment was to be expected. I suddenly felt great tenderness toward Tony, and I smiled freely.

"Well," I said, "you certainly shook up those viruses in your body."

We stared at each other, his expression insisting on calamity, and mine, steadfastly, on a way through the strange, flawed space between us.

"Who knows?" I continued. "Maybe you knocked them around so much that you dazed them, confused them! Maybe you made them forget that they're viruses!"

Tony's eyes finally softened, and his brows retreated from the bridge of his nose. He smiled faintly and turned away, repeating, "Shit, man," very softly now.

"Yeah," I persisted, "maybe they just forgot."

Tony smiled broadly. Then, after a few seconds, his expression acutely changed and he looked at me with great suspicion. I thought, Oh, no, he's going to go off on me again.

For several moments we remained locked in each other's gaze. And then, finally, his face cast a clear expression of wonderment, and he said, "Well, you're nuts, too, aren't you?"

I was so relieved that he had noticed. "Yes," I replied delightedly. "A little."

Our laughter became the sound of our connection setting firmly. It joined us in the place of recognizing part of our selves in each other, in a territory beyond the conventional borders that tended to define the topography of patient and physician interactions. I think Tony could see that, at least, I could sense the landscape of his craziness, that I understood how lives—like my own—seeped through the porous boundaries of "normal behavior." Most of all, I think it comforted him to see me unafraid (finally) to meet him somewhere in the frightening territory of his dementia.

When I said good-bye to him minutes later, he was still sitting on the floor, shaking his head.

"Yeah, good-bye, I guess," he replied calmly. "You're crazy. See you later."

Lamentations
1985–1990

In the realm of decline, in momentary days,
be the crystal cup that shattered even while it rang.

Be, knowing the great void where all things begin,
the infinite source of your inmost vibration,
so that, this once, you may give it your perfect assent.

—RAINER MARIA RILKE, THE SONNETS TO ORPHEUS – II, 13

The first death I attended on the AIDS ward was Lana's. One final shower of bacteria had burst through her bloodstream and claimed her life in a semiprivate room with a faded watercolor print of wildflowers above her bed. In the hour before her death, in the empty space surrounding her, I sometimes paced, sometimes sat, sometimes took her damp, bony hand in mine. When she ceased breathing, I drew a deep breath of my own and slowly exhaled into the room, noting the unopened Coke can and contraband Tupperware containers on her bed stand. I pronounced her name and released her hand.

Throughout the night following her death, I continued to see Lana's hollow-eyed expression that had remained steadfast during her long hospitalization. I continued to feel the considerable and uncomfortable empty space that had surrounded her hospital bed. How, I wondered, had Lana experienced that space? Was there something roaming within it that disturbed or saddened her? That had called her life to the anesthesia of heroin? Or had it always been emptiness itself that haunted? Could she have imagined or wished for something born in relationship to another human being that might have filled the space surrounding her: a caring friend, concerned family members, a lover's sadness, a spoken prayer, a mother's embrace? But Lana had remained isolated throughout her weeks of dying, and, at death, she was unclaimed by the world.

Lana's death was the first I had experienced during my medical practice, independent of academic faculty or other colleagues among whom issues of patient care are generally shared and outcomes are distributed. Her isolation—and mine—disturbed me, and I did not sleep well. In the middle of the night I threw my terry-cloth robe over my shoulders and walked the hall to my living room. There I pulled a dusty, blank canvas journal from a bookshelf and entered Lana's name and the date. The black ink from my felt-tip pen seeped its darkness into the page, leaving fuzzy, ill-defined edges on the letters. In a separate spiral notebook, I wrote briefly of Lana's death and her medical diagnoses and her first words to me: "I'm really just waiting to die, is all." This was a quiet, personal ceremony in the privacy of my small apartment.

What followed Lana's name in my notebooks over the next five years were the names of more and more people who died on our AIDS ward. The names of many patients who expired at their homes or in nursing facilities are missing; also, by early 1990, I had ceased recording the deaths.

In late 1995, soon after beginning to reshape some of my journal entries and patient records into stories and personal essays, I attended a musical performance by a Celtic singer named Nóírín Ní Riain. Her concert was held in a spacious church in Berkeley, California. Having arrived late, I sat in the last pew, exhausted from a tedious eleven-hour workday at the health-maintenance organization where I had been employed for five years.

I felt sorely disappointed that I could not see the performer from my seat. After the first few songs, I decided to relax and abandon my neck-craning attempts to view Nóírín on stage. So I closed my eyes and leaned back against the wooden pew. I heard her voice sail gracefully and majestically throughout the church, echoing off the high-arched ceiling, and I soon felt myself carried by it. I thought of Jay and our goldfish and the sun-shafted trails of the redwood forest. As I traveled with Nóírín's voice, I began to think about the names in my notebooks, and I started to recall the faces belonging to those names.

When her song ended, Nóírín told us a story about her recent trip to Bosnia. She and friends had visited an old army barracks that soldiers had delegated for the temporary shelter of displaced women and children. The barracks were huge, crude, cold metal huts. The women and children were hungry and had little clothing. The singer described feeling herself struck helpless by the utter despair in the refugees' faces and the language barrier that separated her from them.

She found herself standing before them with only her voice and a few hand-held instruments; and so she began to sing. Soon the women and children joined her in the choruses. Nóírín told how together they transformed the cold, dark place with their voices. Their harmonies filled the vast, airless spaces under the arched metal ceiling, and the walls of the barracks vibrated.

Months later, Nóirín and her troupe returned to Bosnia to revisit the women and children in the barracks. However, when they arrived, they found the barracks empty; the refugees had been evacuated again, in a great hurry, and their new whereabouts were unknown. All that remained were remnants of those peoples' suffered existence: a child's toy, a torn sock, a set of keys, a prayer book. Wondering how to understand the seemingly senseless and enormous pain of their war-torn lives, wondering how to bear the tremendous grief in her heart, Nóirín stood in the dark center of the huge, barren place and began to sing once again. She sang a lamentation until it filled the awful emptiness inside the barracks and vibrated its walls once more. She said that this was all she knew she could do—to bear witness to those peoples' suffering and to the unfathomable tragedy of their lives.

And then she sang that same lamentation for us in the church. As I listened, I silently wept. I felt her song resonating inside me. I envisioned my book of names, and my red plastic milk crate filled with remnants of my patients' lives. I heard Nóirín's lamentation vibrating the walls of our AIDS ward, sounding in its deathbeds—a deep resonant reverberation that joined us to the refugees torn from the barracks, to a history of human suffering that bypassed understanding, to the mysterious place where even the gods wept.

Sometimes, in the midst of incomprehensible suffering, there seems little more that we can do but lament, grieve, and so bear witness.

~ 1985 ~

Lana F.   Johnny S.
Ed H.

~ 1986 ~

Rafael N.	Robert M.
Ross B.	Kenneth J.
Mabel H.	David P.
Craig B.	Daniel I.
Anthony G.	Kevin H.
Franklin H.	Thomas T.
Norman S.	Albert L.
Gary K.	James D.
John C.	Richard S.
Dennis S.	Harry F.
Martin C.	Claude R.
Richard H.	Philip C.
Anthony C.	David T.
William T.	Curtis W.
Robert I.	Joseph W.
Donald P.	Ralph H.
Henry K.	Clarence W.
John M.	Ronald B.
Robert S.	Stephen G.
Paul B.	Danny P.
Kenneth D.	William C.
Lionel C.	Charles B.
Anthony A.	Jeffrey D.

~ 1987 ~

Conrad V.

Karl M.

Charles B.

Bobby H.

Richard C

Marvin R.

Paul S.

Terrance S.

William C.

Charles W.

Randy D.

George D.

David B.

Dario M.

David M.

Michael D.

Deborah S.

Tyler A.

Paul O.

Ed M.

Douglas F.

Elaina W.

Larry T.

Oscar C.

Tua S.

Terry V.

George M.

Edward G.

Donald J.

Tom T.

Robert B.

Michael A.

Melvin N.

Thomas L.

Jonathan W.

Vernon N.

John H.

Leander D.

June K.

Rodger B.

Alan D.

Shawn L.

Robert B.

Paul G.

James H.

Louis G.

Oliver B.

James B.

Spencer L.

David F.

Terry R.

Thomas F.

Ken S.

Eric L.

Stephen M.

Carroll B.

Michael A.

~ 1988 ~

Victoria H.

Stephen L.

Arthur C.

Antonio R.

Frank T.

Daniel V.

Kevin C.

Edward J.

John S.

Donald A.

Kim O.

Vaughn C.

Rick S.

Robert L.

David M.

Ronald G.

Dennis N.

Leslie D.

Gordon M.

Ronald H.

David R.

Jack H.

Markalan J.

Eric D.

Josef R.

Joseph R.

John F.

Yaya A.

Steven O.

Danny J.

Kenneth B.

Dennis K.

Medland R.

Viola S.

Richard O.

Gary F.

Robin H.

Stephen S.

William M.

Kandi L.

Charles W.

Gary M.

Albert A.

Victoria G.

Ira D.

Keith B.

Lee A.

Norman B.

Gary O.

Edward C.

John N.

Kristofer F.

Harold J.

Charles C.

~ 1989 ~

Orlando G.

Allen S.

Fred K.

Jose H.

Robert J.

George R.

Glen R.

Stephen W.

Christopher T.

Alan A.

Graham G.

Rufus H.

Bernard W.

Scott C.

Benjamin A.

Paul B.

Harold Y.

Edward B.

Gus B.

David F.

George M.

Willie N.

Elia Q.

Michael R.

William A.

James H.

Jerry M.

Scott M.

Charles L.

Herbert W.

Stephen B.

Jose P.

Roger P.

George A.

Donald G.

David K.

Willie N.

Richard H.

Gary C.

John B.

Lee T.

Lorena D.

Richard H.

~ 1990 ~

Curtis G.	*Brian B.*
Gregory M.	*Jose A.*
Earl B.	*Jim L.*
Robert	*Raymond M.*
Johanna G.	*Thomas M.*
Julie C.	*William R.*

Leaving AIDS

We shall not cease from exploration
And the end of all our exploring
Will be to arrive where we started
And know the place for the first time.
—T. S. Eliot, Little Gidding

My leaving the AIDS ward was a confused affair. For months, I struggled with an exhausting uncertainty about leaving my job. The solidity of each "definite decision" I made—to go or to stay—provided only a hard surface for me to bump against and fall back from, into yet another bruised perspective in which new flaws in my reasoning were revealed.

This terrible uncertainty began during my fifth year on the ward. In January of 1990 I wrote in my journal about my "exhaustion with death." I had become so ensconced within the medical and sociopolitical world of AIDS work that I had begun to feel alienated from the larger body of general medical practice and the world of personal experience beyond disease and death. I was beginning to forget the ways that organs normally aged with time, the somatic intricacies of diabetes, issues of women's health care, renal and cardiac and rheumatologic medicine. And I realized that I was beginning to forget how to live my own life.

During my years on the ward, I had developed a sobriety about life that tended to mute my experiences of joy or pleasure. I had found it difficult to join in the small talk of everyday life, the social communication essential for personal relationships. Friends' talk of their day-to-day experiences often seemed small and irrelevant when set against my constant mental backdrop of death and suffering. My social circle constricted over time, and, in 1989, I faced the termination of a long-term relationship in which my mind and heart could no longer alight.

The landscape of AIDS work had also changed. In the beginning, large segments of society and the medical profession had refused to work with AIDS patients; those who did become involved were generally drawn to the work through a heightened sense of personal or political commitment. In later years, the epidemic expanded and evolved in ways that provided opportunities for many. I do not mean to imply that workers with maligned hearts or greedy intellects infiltrated the landscape but, rather, that the motivations for entering AIDS work simply changed: they sometimes reflected a desire to establish an academic career, procure a grant, or distinguish one's self within an increasingly high-profile social organization. AIDS clinics sprung up and competed with one another for patients, often invoking divisive politics in their marketing ventures. Insurance companies and businesses banked on the epidemic.

Within this milieu, I waited for a revelation that would help me resolve my feelings about my work. I sensed the presence of a wholly illuminating truth existing just beyond my reach. My frustrating attempts to grasp this truth and my continued uncertainty wore me down and depressed me.

In mid-January of 1990, I stopped recording patients' deaths in my journal. I felt as though I had reached some critical limit with death, as though it could be measured or weighed, like potatoes or melons.

I had also begun to make lists in my personal journal, rival columns of "pros" and "cons" to help me decide about my job. The cons advocating my leave included these: the constant suffering and death, the narrowed spectrum of medical practice, the turgid psychosocial dilemmas, no job benefits or security, the changed landscape of AIDS work. Ironically, the pros column also included the first three cons: care of the dying was an amazingly rich and rewarding experience; possession of expertise within a circumscribed field of medicine was comforting; and, perhaps because my personal life off the AIDS ward had become so small, the intense emotional aspects of my patients' complicated lives proved compelling.

By March I began using words like *amputated* and *unlived* to describe my personal life. While I experienced immediacy and intensity in my one-on-one relationships with patients, I also felt that a mysterious distance separated me from my work. I felt as though I were operating unevenly on two levels of experience, as though represented by the iconography of a fresco: In the foreground, my personal relationships with patients stood out clearly, while, recessed behind them, was the large background of medical practice. In the intervening distance separating the two spanned the elusive truth I could not see.

To my relief, by April, my depression and frustration began to recede, devolving, I thought, through simple natural attrition. By default, I found myself yielding to my uncertainty that soon lost its paralyzing effect and became a mobilizing force beckoning me into the world beyond the AIDS ward, to the mysterious distance between my personal experience and my profession.

Armed with little more than my intuition and a trust that what I didn't know would prove to be a reliable guide, I left the ward in June of 1990. I placed several hundred medical records, dozens of stories, two personal journals, my catalog of patients' deaths, and voluminous collections of newspaper and magazine clippings into a red plastic milk crate and several cardboard boxes and stored them in my basement.

In 1999, I tenderly remember the young physician who, in 1985, abandoned her academic career with hopes of entering a commonplace medical practice. Her vital statistics were these: she was thirty-two years old, white, born in a county hospital to an Irish-Catholic family with eleven siblings near Detroit, Michigan; she weighed one hundred twenty pounds, wore corduroys and tennis shoes to work and, sometimes, a white coat. She was board certified in internal medicine and rheumatology, and her professional goal had been that of serving indigent populations in a county hospital setting.

How shocked she was to find that she had stumbled into a job at a county hospital that led, instead, into an AIDS epicenter. Much of the internal medicine she had learned over many difficult years would be rendered irrelevant; her three years of fellowship acquiring expertise in arthritis and autoimmune disorders would prove almost superfluous. Most of her patients would be men, while her heart and her politics had always steered her toward a medical practice serving poor women and families. Since all her AIDS patients would be hospitalized, most would be dying (at that time the average life expectancy was thirty-five weeks after the "AIDS pneumonia," pneumocystis, was diagnosed). In 1985, working with the medical uncertainties of AIDS involved, for the physician, an often stressful working-from-the-seat-of-her-pants, taking necessary but blatant risks with human lives. It was dealing with patients' families whose personal or religious judgments about homosexuality and AIDS had to be reconciled quickly at their son's deathbed, often unsatisfactorily. In 1985, no celebrity wore a red ribbon on his or her lapel; and it was the first year that President Reagan publicly uttered the word *AIDS.*

I want to tell her that if she proceeds with her new job, her heart will be broken a thousand times and she will experience darkness in new and difficult ways. I want to tell her to hang on, because the years she will spend on the ward will prove to be the most meaningful and extraordinary years of her personal and professional life. I find that I can't tell her yet, not now, about the cancers she will have in her near future.

And I see that young physician slowly yield, bend, and shape in ways she never imagined. I see her allowing herself to be tossed and shaken by the strange new illnesses of AIDS, the repetitive deaths, the shocking ways that people lived their lives, the incredibly varied configurations of families, the creative expressions of sexuality, the alien subculture of drug users, the maddening politics of public health.

After leaving the ward in 1990, I began a new job in one of the country's largest health maintenance organizations. My outpatient clinic schedule was fractured into fifteen-minute appointments throughout the day. I practiced medicine in a rigidly regimented and exhausting pace, resurrecting my old, rusty expertise in internal medicine and rheumatology. I was removed from the wide-open possibilities of personal experience that had been offered to me at bedsides on the AIDS ward, from the intimacies with patients that accompany life-threatening illness, from the natural ebb and flow of work directed by spontaneous expressions of patients' lives and deaths. The contrast with my old job was stunning. My new work felt like a factory line of lives presented to me in rapid-sequence sound bites.

When, five years later, in May of 1995, my friend asked what I had stored inside the red milk crate and adjacent boxes that, for years, had laid in the center of my basement, my response was one of great sadness, remembering both my patients and the uncomfortable distance between my profession and my lived personal experience. I had never found the elusive truth which had beckoned me to explore that distance between me and my work. In fact, sadly, that distance had expanded during my five years at the HMO: Subordinating the realm of the personal to the fast-paced mechanical delivery of medical care had only served to make me feel more split off, pushed into the backdrop of the fresco, into the traditional narrative of the physician as manager of bodies and facts and knowledge, as observer, as technician.

But my friend's question also ignited in me a suspicion that the truth I had sought was hovering nearby. That suspicion vibrated with hope that, after many years now, that truth, once illuminated, could integrate my lived experience and my profession.

As I sat on my basement floor and read of Marvin and Lana and Jay and Elton and others, I also read of some strange young woman who was with them as physician, confidant, cook, explorer, stumbler, sprinter, shopper, referee, mother, counselor, ranch hand, comforter, foil, traveler, historian, seeker, doubter, friend, fish custodian, sentry. I read story after story the first night, desperately trying to define the young woman with evidence of her existence. Amid unmeasurable grief for the deaths and sufferings of my patients in the crate, I also grieved for the life of that young physician who was me.

What I now believe happened to that young physician was this: She had existed outside language. On the ward, as a physician, her interior domain found no mirror in the conventional imagery of medical practice. While she was often studious, rational, and knowledgeable, she was also fallible and vulnerable and uncertain; she sometimes used intuition— hers or her patients—for diagnostic guidance; her official medical treatments sometimes meant taking patients on rides through the park or bringing them fresh baked goods.

She was a woman who entered medical school in 1976 having never before seen a female physician. She began to practice at a time when it was usual for men (and some women) to scoff at the idea of a woman providing good medical care. In 1983, having completed three rigorous years of a residency program in Chicago, her commencement ceremony featured a female stripper as the evening's main entertainment.

And this woman and physician was also a lesbian, someone whose identity was overtly pathologized by the medical profession and represented in psychiatric literature as "deviant." She often cared for patients who made homophobic comments in her presence.

She was someone who, as a physician, was rather invisible as a person.

She had not seen her experience reflected in the traditional physician narratives; in fact, she was excluded by them. As such, she felt a destabilizing distance between her reality and her work. She stored her work in boxes and crates and journals that no one else would see and she felt the depersonalizing effects of her new corporate job further increase the distance between her and her profession. She continued to see her interior realm pushed further and further away from her work.

But, finally, the woman and the physician discovered each other. From across the distance separating them, they spoke. What they finally realized—what I realized—was that the integration of my lived experience and my profession would require that I claim it into existence. That I make the connection with words.

By writing these stories, I have written my life.

EPILOGUE

My Cancer and the AIDS Quilt

*Some uncomprehended law holds us at a point
of contradiction where we have no choice,
where we do not like that which we love,
where good and bad are inseparable partners impossible
to tell apart, and where we—heartbroken and ecstatic—can only
resolve the conflict by taking it into our hearts.
This used to be called being in the hands of God.*
—FLORIDA SCOTT-MAXWELL, THE MEASURE OF MY DAYS

On October 15, 1996, at 8:30 in the morning, I mailed the completed manuscript for this book to my agent in New York. I was determined to finish it before leaving for Paris hours later that same day; I had planned two weeks in France as a celebration to inaugurate my year's sabbatical from work, my venture into midlife "philosopause."

My partner and I had packed, the house was prepared, the garden sprinklers were programmed for our absence, and the newspapers would wait our leave. The taxi was scheduled to arrive at noon. Our flight on Air France would depart the San Francisco airport at 2:45.

At 10:20 A.M., only two things—both phone calls—remained on my long checklist of things to do. I first phoned the pathology department where I worked to

obtain my uterine biopsy report from one of my colleagues; I had experienced technical difficulty trying to
access the report from my surgeon twice during the previous week. We all expected the biopsy to be normal, since I
was forty-three years old, thin, perimenopausal, and had
experienced only two months of slight intermenstrual
bleeding. Fingering the plane tickets, waiting for the
pathologist to come to the phone, congratulating myself
for finishing this manuscript, I sat elated at my desk; an
entire year, free of twelve-hour workdays, open for self-
exploration, lay ahead.

At 10:22, the pathologist spoke the word *cancer* and
my world turned upside down. Immediately. Completely.
That I could be transported in one second from a healthy
life literally poised on the doorstep of a midlife exploration to a life interrupted by uterine cancer seemed
unimaginable, unreal. Three weeks later, during surgery,
the discovery that I also harbored a separate ovarian
cancer would amplify my astonishment immeasurably.

Several weeks after my surgery, I sat in the San
Francisco office of an oncologist who was expressing her
disagreement with the previous consultant's optimistic
assessment of my cancer. She thought it likely that, instead
of two separate cancers, I had only uterine, and that it had
spread to my ovary. In my situation, it would have been
"preferable" to have two independent cancers without
detectable spread of either. She also recommended more
severe and extensive chemotherapy in addition to prolonged, high-dose progesterone treatment.

As a physician for seventeen years, I had watched
metastatic cancer pull many of my own patients' lives into
suffering and death. As medical director of an AIDS ward
for five years, I had stood the bedside death watch fre-

quently. Suddenly, with the specialist's words—"I think it's metastatic cancer"—I walked through the thin veil that had always separated me from my "living dying" patients.

My new membership in the world of the living dying happened so fast, so quietly, and so unceremoniously that I found it difficult to believe that it had really happened. But for my healing surgical wounds, I felt completely well. I lingered a few moments in the drab, cluttered office of this methodical, prosaic physician and waited for something to mark my transition—even a stirring of my own emotions. But no official spokesperson from the dying came to welcome me, and no celestial light show broke into the room. Which consultant was right?

As I exited her office, my numbness began to thaw just enough to allow my despair to surface. I then entered the clinic elevator, feeling suddenly removed from the living world of people crowded around me. Although my partner stood less than an inch away, I felt as though I were already leaving her.

As very slow elevators seem wont to do, this one stopped on every floor of the towering clinic building, admitting more and more of the world that I feared I would soon have to leave. At one stop, a pixilated elderly woman in a cocked brimmed hat and oversized wool coat finessed her way through the compact crowd to take position near me and declare loudly, "You have such beautiful hair! You should thank your parents for that."

I exchanged glances with my partner, and then turned back to the woman whose toothless grin persisted. "Thank you," I replied, "but it looks like I'll be losing it soon."

"Why?" she asked perplexed, attracting the attention of others.

"I have cancer," I replied in a wobbly, cracked voice. "The medicine they'll give me will make my hair fall out." This peculiar occasion marked the first time I had announced publicly that I had cancer, and the words barely made it out of my mouth. I had been trying not to cry since leaving the specialist's office.

The woman placed her gnarled hand on my arm and said, "Oh, that's just not fair. God won't let that happen to such beautiful hair." Moments later, the elevator door opened to the lobby, and, after smiling at me again, the woman exited, humming "Oh! Susanna." I felt as though I had been "visited" by this woman. As though she had been sent as an emissary to pull me back to the world of the living. Her wonderful strangeness and peculiar kindness allowed my raw and private agony to enter the public domain to be received, however oddly.

My partner and I linked arms and walked two blocks to our car. I had trouble looking at her face and witnessing her grief. I felt like apologizing in advance for abandoning her, for dying in my early forties. But all I could say was "God" or "Oh, my God." Along the way, on the sidewalk, an agitated, muscular man yelled curses as he pummeled the air with clenched fists; a frightened mother dragged her child across the street to avoid the man's frenzied path; a young girl asked me if I wanted to buy roses; and teenagers stood before a store window discussing the relative merits of cotton and polyester.

On the way home we had planned to drive to Planetree, an extensive cancer resource library. But when our car approached the facility, I realized I did not want to see any more medical information. In the few weeks after the surgery that had revealed my tumors, I had been discomforted consistently by all the medical literature I had reviewed, all the scientific studies my colleagues had sent me. None of it seemed to address the considerable residual parts of me remaining after the removal of my uterus and ovaries and appendix and omentum and lymph nodes and overt cancers.

"Let's drive to Grace Cathedral instead," I suggested. "I'd like to walk the labyrinth."

Within minutes we stood on the cathedral's outdoor plaza in which its labyrinth was embedded. The one-third-mile meandering path had been modeled after the eleven-circuit labyrinth built between 1194 and 1220 in Chartres Cathedral in southern France. Based on a circle, the universal symbol of wholeness and unity, it invited one to partake in a walking meditation through inter-loped spirals as a metaphorical journey through life to the divine.

Five weeks earlier, my partner and I had walked the origi-nal Chartres labyrinth during our trip to France. We did so after exploring Paris, often dazed and insomniac, won-dering how extensive my cancer was, for two weeks. I had been a universal supplicant in Paris. I prayed to "any god willing to listen." I prayed to the saints I had prayed to as a child in the Catholic churches of Detroit. I frequently recited the twenty-third Psalm. I read and reread June Singer's *A Gnostic Book of Hours* and Rilke's *Book of Hours*. I routinely practiced my meditation. I repeated the prayer a patient of mine had prayed for me as she sat in her wheelchair and held my hand, bidding me farewell for my year's sabbatical: "Dear God—and there really is one, Dr. Scannell—take Dr. Scannell into your hands this year, watch over her, and bring her back safely."

During our second week in France, physically and emotionally exhausted, we arranged a day trip to Chartres. Upon entering its ancient cathedral, I found myself drawn to the timeworn labyrinth in the nave's west end. First stepping into the 861-foot walking path, I was surprised to discover how quickly I sensed that I would somehow be comforted. Further along the labyrinth, I began to feel the awful weight of my private agony shift, as though it were being shared with others. Gradually, my grief seemed to "normalize" as it resonated with the grief of hundreds of thousands of other supplicants who, over centuries, had walked the same path, searching for meaning, invoking grace, praying for help to accept their troubled lives and deaths.

The clanking bell of the cable car mounting California Street, the discordant symphony of truck and automobile noises filling noon-time San Francisco, and the lively conversation of grounds keepers began to fade as I moved through the labyrinth at Grace Cathedral. I felt incrementally grounded with each foot placed firmly on the labyrinth path. As I walked, I gradually understood that my despair about the uncertainty of my diagnosis was a surface one, reflecting the deeper underlying uncertainty— about when I would die.

I had been in this place of sober wonderment many times before with my AIDS patients who had struggled to accept the unknowable and the mysterious that hovered around their imminent deaths. Because I had visited this place so often, I felt less a stranger and less alone within it.

Toward the center of the labyrinth, the uncertainty about my cancer became less formidable as I increasingly accepted uncertainty itself. Coursing through intertwined spirals, sensing pattern and relationship of one to the other and to the greater collective whole, I began to feel comforted again by experiencing my grief as part of the human condition, my prospective death as part of the divine natural order, that all life led to death.

When I reached the center, the midway resting place in the walking meditation, I cried finally; and I asked for help to accept the uncertainty of my life and the certainty of my eventual death. I remembered many patients, many friends and family, who had died; I felt them holding me inside the natural order, the universal human labyrinth, the great mystery of death that belongs to us all.

After completing our walk, I entered Grace Cathedral, wishing to sit a few quiet moments in its still, cavernous center. But, beyond its majestic doors, I discovered an orchestra assembling for a Yuletide practice session. I considered leaving, but was so fatigued by my recent surgery that I decided to rest a few moments in a back pew. Seated there, I closed my eyes and tried to meditate.

But loud distracting noises filled the cathedral—the scuff of shoes, the chafe of folding chairs against the wood floor, the clack and click of music stands rallying, the traffic of buses and cable cars outside. I finally decided to leave. But, with my eyes still closed, I heard a metallic tapping and an immediate quiet that followed. When I opened my eyes, the orchestra began to play, filling the church with a soft reedy music enlarging seconds later with the silky sounds of violins. The music's beauty transported me from my fragile grief and solitude. Although I did not recognize the music, it seemed familiar, as though remembered by my soul, as though transcending time.

My eyes slowly accommodated to the cathedral's dark interior. Sacred objects hanging on the walls, religious statues poised in nooks and crannies, flowers set on the altar, and other people situated in other pews gradually emerged. As the orchestra continued to play and as my vision adjusted, I noticed that, hanging from one wall, was a large panel from the AIDS quilt.

I stood up and walked the side aisles to view the rest of the cathedral walls. More quilt sections were on display, with more names, more names, more names of men and women who had died from AIDS. I walked the display path as though it were another labyrinth meditation, experiencing again the proximity of death and the transience of life.

I stopped at a panel commemorating one of my patients. Touching it, remembering him, managing to say his name aloud through my grief, I imagined my own panel stitched next to his. Then I envisioned a quilt containing a panel from each and every person who had ever lived, each panel bearing the name and tableau of one person's life. People who had walked the Chartres labyrinth seven hundred years before, masses of Pakistanis swept under floods, Irish families starved to death during the potato famine, children fatally injured at traffic stops, elderly women who died in their sleep...

Later, when we drove home, I kept imagining this quilt with its countless panels each uniquely rendered and, finally, stitched in common. Its fabric that of memory, warm and richly textured. The weave of natural order its reliable workmanship. This massive quilt a comforter that each of us, in our time, with our various religious beliefs and our disparate identities, will reach for, like a universal prayer before dying.

SELECTED BOOKS FROM CLEIS PRESS

A Fragile Union
NEW AND SELECTED WRITINGS

Joan Nestle

"Joan Nestle's work has always embodied a very large vision. This vibrant new collection burns with the generosity and courage of her spirit, the beauty of her writing—on both pleasure and pain—and the distinction of her critical intelligence. On the eve of the twenty-first century, *A Fragile Union* is a powerful, tensile span between past and future."—*ADRIENNE RICH*

"Joan Nestle represents, for each of us, courage, intelligence, beauty, a sense of conviction and humility... She has revolutionized history, both the craft and in the facts of life." —*BLANCHE WIESEN COOK, AUTHOR, Eleanor Roosevelt, 1844-1933*

$14.95   ISBN: 1-57344-040-X

The Little School
TALES OF DISAPPEARANCE AND SURVIVAL
SECOND EDITION

Alicia Partnoy. Preface by Julia Alvarez

Told in a series of tales that resound in memory like parables, Alicia Partnoy's memoir is proof of the resilience of the human spirit and the healing powers of art. An Argentine student activist, Alicia Partnoy was abducted from her home and taken to a concentration camp where she was tortured, and where many "disappeared" were killed. Her writings were smuggled out of prison and published anonymously in human rights journals.

"As works of art, these stories are *triumphant.*"—*The Sunday Times (London)*

$14.95   ISBN: 1-57344-029-9

I Am My Own Woman
THE OUTLAW LIFE OF CHARLOTTE VON MAHLSDORF,
BERLIN'S MOST DISTINGUISHED TRANSVESTITE

Charlotte von Mahlsdorf. Translated by Jean Hollander

"Move over Quentin Crisp: A naked civil servant is nothing compared with the German boy in a dress…" —*OUT MAGAZINE*

"As a child, Lothar Berfelde loved to wear an apron and polish porcelain. Given his druthers, he would have chosen to live quietly in the 19th century, perhaps as a housekeeper in a well-appointed home near Berlin. Instead, his life took a bumpier course…." —*Time Magazine*

$12.95   ISBN: 1-57344-010-8

On the Rails
A MEMOIR

Linda Niemann. Introduction by Leslie Marmon Silko

On the Rails "is about railroading the way Moby Dick is about whaling…" —*Chicago Sun Times*

"Reads like a travelogue of forbidden places, an adventure story and an erotic fantasy…This is a hot book." —*WENDY CHAPKIS, Women's Review of Books*

$14.95   ISBN: 1-57344-064-7

About the Author

Kate Scannell is an internist, rheumatologist, and
geriatrician, and an Assistant Clinical Professor of
Medicine and the University of California, San Francisco.
She is currently working on a collection of short stories
and a memoir of her experiences with cancer.